Current Approaches

Psychiatry and the Law

Edited by
J J Bradley, V J Harten-Ash
& M L Page

duphar
medical relations

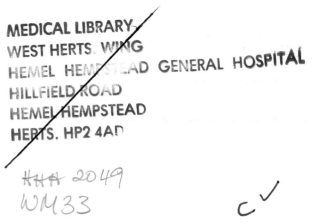
© 1990 Duphar Laboratories Limited

First published 1990

ISBN 1 870678 24 9

Printed in Great Britain by Henry Ling Ltd.,
at the Dorset Press, Dorchester, Dorset

CONTENTS

EDITOR'S FOREWORD

The law as a structured, man-made system intrudes daily into the life of the psychiatrist trying to grapple with the uncertainties and ambiguities of mental disorder. However, even the law with its precision is shy of defining mental disorder, except by breaking it down into the sub-categories of mental illness, mental impairment, severe mental impairment and psychopathic disorder.

Uneasy bed-fellows though they may be at times, the law and psychiatry have to co-exist and communicate, and perhaps learn a little of each others language which hopefully will lead to mutual respect. Both, after all only exist for the good of society, even though the cynical observer might find a long trial on quantum in a compensation case with teams of highly paid lawyers, expert witnesses and an apparently barely disabled plaintiff more symptomatic of human greed rather than justice.

As doctors we only practice by courtesy of the law as administered by the General Medical Council, which does confer a great deal of power upon us, and of course obligations. Likewise the Mental Health Act gives doctors— even quite junior ones, the power to deprive a citizen of his or her liberty for up to 72 hours (under Section 5(2))—a power granted to no other group apart from statutory authorities such as the police. It is, therefore, not surprising that the Mental Health Act of 1983 was drafted so that the rights of the individual should be more adequately safeguarded than in the previous 1959 Act, in terms of detention, treatment and consent. Inevitably this has led to more complicated procedures with a greater sharing of authority and closer monitoring.

Society demands that every effort must be made to preserve the civil liberties of the individual, at the same time requiring protection from the mentally disordered who may be dangerous (though dangerousness is notoriously difficult to predict). Courts increasingly require the recommendations of psychiatrists in criminal proceedings and expect the psychiatric and social services to provide appropriate treatment and supervision for mentally disordered offenders often with inadequate resources, and to some extent act as an agent of the law by providing accommodation for those on remand, regular reports to the Home Office in restricted cases, and notification of drug addiction.

In this age of consumerism civil litigation has escalated and claims for compensation for psychiatric sequelae of accidents, medical negligence, industrial and criminal injuries are made more and more frequently. Most cases never reach open court, but psychiatrists are frequently called upon as experts prior to settlement, while some may be unfortunate enough to find themselves in the witness box trapped between battling advocates for plaintiff and defendant.

At a whole day symposium a panel of medically qualified speakers (some with legal qualifications or experience) addressed a wide range of complex issues relating to the interface of the law and psychiatry. The papers included in this volume bear witness that much valuable information has been disseminated, which is now more widely available thanks to Duphar Medical Relations.

J J BRADLEY
Chairman of Council, Medical Protection Society
Consultant Psychiatrist, Whittington Hospital

THE MENTAL HEALTH ACT—AND WHAT IS NOT IN IT!

Professor Elaine Murphy
Vice Chairman of the Mental Health Act Commission
Professor of Psychogeriatrics
United Medical Schools, Guy's Hospital, London

I joined the Mental Heath Act Commission only 16 months ago. Like most psychiatrists working in the community my experience included 'sectioning' people who needed treatment for psychiatric disorder. At that time I probably shared the common misconceptions that professionals who use the Act have about the Act and the role of the Mental Health Act Commission. This paper will address some of the key issues in relation to treatment and research with mentally incompetent and mentally disordered people that are not dealt with in the Act. I will also mention the arrangements for the Code of Practice.

PRINCIPLES

The Mental Health Act of 1983 and its forebears back in the Lunacy Act of 1845 all emerged from a common concern that individuals who are ill or handicapped in ways that render them incapable of making autonomous decisions are vulnerable. They need special protection to ensure that their treatment and care is warranted, does not fall below a certain standard of practice and that they are protected from unnecessary or ill treatment. On the other hand there is equally strong concern that vulnerable individuals should receive the care and treatment they require whether or not they understand the need for it and that the best available care should be afforded to them. This balancing of principles must underlie all decisions when treating mentally disordered people—a balance of rights and duties. It is obvious that there is scope for conflict between these two principles which has been at the root of many anxieties and resentments that professionals have expressed about the recent 1983 Act. This may be fuelled by the suspicion that campaigners for the Act did not understand the needs of severely mentally ill people and were perhaps grinding axes to fight in battles other than those concerned with mentally disordered people.

It is now six years since the Act was implemented and most of us have accepted the need to have our own professional freedoms curtailed in the interests of patients at large. The Act actually gives us new and more secure ways forward for treating mentally ill people who cannot give consent or who refuse treatment. Dr Harper's paper will address Part IV of the Act and some of the parts of the Act which have created most difficulty. I will therefore concentrate on those areas that affect general psychiatric practice.

The Mental Health Act is only concerned with a small corner of the framework of legislation which affects our treatment of mentally ill people. It has to be seen against the backdrop of English common law; the common ground of

1

precedents against which all doctors, nurses and other professionals treat and care for patients, whether they are physically or mentally disordered. Many issues concerning consent to treatment of incapable patients which crop up in our day to day practice have never been the subject of court cases and there is no legal precedent on which to decide how to deal with the issues, particularly treatment of physical illness in incapable patients. We therefore seek in vain for legal guidance. As Mental Health Act Commissioners travelling round the country we find that the law is being divined in what one of my colleagues called 'multi-disciplinary prayer groups'. This, I believe, is the only way at present until the professions, the Mental Health Act Commission, the Law Commission and, if necessary, the courts agree on the way forward.

Let me cite three cases that have come to my attention recently as examples of the problems. Mr Brown is a 68 year old man with a paranoid psychosis of long standing, who is in a psychiatric hospital where he has lived for 35 years; he smokes like a chimney, as do many of our long-stay patients, and over the last 5 years has developed severe peripheral vascular disease. He is in considerable pain and cannot walk more than a few steps. A surgeon has advised that reconstructive surgery may benefit him substantially, but it is a risky procedure. Mr Brown says that his bad leg is caused by German soldiers who have been controlling him for the last 40 years. They must be placated and he is quite frightened of doing anything that might upset them; he feels that an operation may interfere with their plans for him. He neither comprehends the problem from which he suffers or its implications nor the risks and benefits of treatment. His only relative is an older sister who lives many miles away and rarely visits. She feels her responsibilities to care for him very deeply and she thinks he ought to have the operations that are being proposed. Neither the surgeon nor the psychiatrist has a clear way forward. Who is to make the decision and on what grounds?

In my second case the unit general manager for services for mentally handicapped people and their psychiatrist were concerned about the assessment of deafness in residents of a mental handicap hospital and the provision of hearing aids. The ENT specialist felt that he could carry out appropriate tests under general anaesthetic and substantially improve the hearing of a number of the long-stay residents. The anaesthetist was unwilling to become involved because the patients could not give consent to the anaesthetic. Who is to make this decision, and on what grounds?

And the third case concerns F, a mentally handicapped woman who is resident in a mental handicap hospital who has formed a sexual relationship with another patient. Both the consultant team and the family would like to have her sterilised. The Court of Appeal decided that the court had jurisdiction over such cases as these and recently the Law Lords have upheld that decision whereby the sterilisation can proceed. Unfortunately, they have not as yet given any reasons behind their judgment.

It is clear that we require a system which allows us to make appropriate judgments in these three cases, which does not always depend upon resort to the courts because these are practical problems facing clinicians every day.

The Government has asked the Law Commission to look into this question of inability to consent in the incapable subject and the Mental Health Act Commission has also attempted to design a hierarchy of safeguards, published in 1985 as a discussion document 'Consent to Treatment'. The Mental Handicap Section of the College of Psychiatrists has made some suggestions for a way forward specifically in cases of sterilisation. The professionals and both Commissions must unite to produce options for a way forward to create practical guidance for day to day practice.

I would like to propose some practical ways of weighing up the options for incompetent subjects.

(1) The beliefs of the patients and their cultural group, or perhaps the former beliefs of elderly people, and the views of relatives, close friends and supporters must be considered.

(2) The likely benefits versus the outcome of inaction.

(3) Whether the patient is actively co-operative or able to co-operate with the procedure,

(4) The risks, the discomfort and nuisance of the procedure

(5) The long-term benefits and disbenefits.

All these must be taken into account. But having used these criteria, how do we reach the decision? There is no simple answer, but I think it is possible to develop safeguards. An obvious one is the agreement of the nearest relative. Of course a relative cannot give consent, but in most cases one would wish the system to involve the agreement of the nearest relative. That is an important aspect which is enshrined in much of the Mental Health Act, that we are concerned with the view of the nearest relative who knows the patient. I think it also helps if the decision is made in a multi-disciplinary fashion by those who are caring for the patient at the time. It is particularly important in long-stay hospitals where the disciplines involved include nurses, psychologist, occupational therapist, even the domestics on the ward at times, who may know the patients better than anybody else, the doctor being only one of a number of people and one who only sees the patient every now and again. I believe there is also merit in formally recording a multi-disciplinary decision.

It has been suggested that a decision could be made by an appointed panel of lay and professional members not directly concerned with care. That is a possibility, but it might be cumbersome unless there was a statutory committee convened within each district to deal with such questions. This could be a way of safeguarding the patient. Independent professional second opinion has also been suggested. Again this is a cumbersome and expensive procedure. It would require new legislation for this to be enacted and I am not sure that this would be a good way forward. I think that a multi-disciplinary, local based approach would provide sufficient safeguards for most care and treatment procedures if formalised into an agreed policy and made explicit.

Lastly, of course, there is resort to the courts to set precedents, but this is a slow and difficult procedure. I would suggest that we need formalised safeguards in a hierarchy to enable us to deal with problems. A protocol which is acceptable to all of us could be created.

3

What else is not in the Mental Health Act? People ring the Commission every day with queries which fall into three categories. There are queries about the Mental Health Act itself, which suggest that some people have not grasped what the Act says. Secondly, there are questions about good practice and the practical operation of the Act; these questions fall under the Code of Practice, such as when to use Section 2 and Section 3 for someone who is being recurrently re-admitted. Thirdly, there are questions of interpretation of the law, which the Mental Health Act Commission is at present not able to do. Where the case is clear advice can be given, but often extremely complex individual cases lie behind the query and the Mental Health Act Commission cannot give professional legal advice off the cuff. Having been on the phoning end I can understand how frustrating it can be that while the Commission was set up to oversee the Mental Health Act, it cannot give legal guidance on how it should operate. Recently the Commission has decided that its policy should be to respond to enquiries where it can, but to stress that the response is a Commission view and that it is for the courts to provide definitive interpretation of the Act. Professionals should seek guidance from their local legal advisers in appropriate cases. In the first instance this should be the District or Regional legal advisory service who may not have specialist knowledge of the Mental Health Act but they can direct the clinician or manager to a specialist firm of solicitors for advice.

At a recent historic meeting of the Commission it was decided to recommend to the Secretary of State that the Commission would cease to operate in three regions with a view to moving towards centralising our offices and functions. This is in order that the Commission can become unified in its policies and ensure that the policy that is being proselytised at the periphery on visits is co-ordinated centrally. This will create a more unified and consistent policy across the country thereby attempting to make uniform the advice to practitioners while at the same time recognising that we cannot give full legal advice.

THE CODE OF PRACTICE

Most psychiatrists are aware of the sorry saga of the draft code. The first was produced by the Commission and it contains a great deal of good advice. Unfortunately it was long, it was controversial and the profession felt it was unacceptable. It is interesting that as the Commission travels round the country it is the first draft code which still sits in ward offices, and I think people are using it to find advice. The second draft was produced by professional advisers within the Department of Health and that was approved by the Royal Colleges; I personally think that it was 'content free'. It provided no practical guidance and was no more than a commentary on the Act. The Department of Health tried to produce a document which was acceptable to everybody. The Department of Health has now launched the definitive working group to produce the Code of Practice to be laid before Parliament this autumn. So it has now taken 6 years to produce this Code of Practice. It must be a practical document, a readable handbook that practitioners can work from daily. The working group includes four clinicians and managers with extensive practical experience with the Act. Also the members are largely drawn from outside the Department. If the resulting document does not in some way disturb the Royal Colleges and if MIND and other voluntary organisations do not criticise it for not being tough enough, then we shall have failed. If everybody is happy, we shall almost certainly have got it wrong. On the other hand we shall also have failed if somebody then has to write an explanatory commentary on the Code of Practice. The main work will be finished by the end of July 1989.

RESEARCH

Lastly I want to mention research with incompetent subjects, another issue which is not contained in the Act. In 1986 the Commission issued a discussion document on consent to research with incompetent subjects, which generated extensive debate and was heavily criticised by academic psychiatrists. It was an extremely well written document in the sense that it highlighted all the issues and analysed the problems very well. Thinking has now moved on and there are a number of possible ways forward. The Medical Research Council is currently discussing this issue and hopes to publish guidance soon. The issues are as follows:

— Under what circumstances, if ever, is research with incompetent subjects possible?

— If there are any subjects where it is justified, how may a decision be reached for individual subjects which safeguards the rights of those individuals?

Again there are no easy answers. The current constitution of District Ethics Committees is not sufficient safeguard in itself. I think there are a number of ways forward and safeguards, which could actually be incorporated into our daily practice in a formalised way. Ethics Committee approval is amongst the most important. An important question to ask is whether the research can be carried out on competent subjects. Obviously studies on patients with long standing schizophrenia or dementia cannot. Agreement by nearest relatives to the involvement of an individual must be important. Agreement by separately convened panels of lay and professional members to consider individual incompetent subjects and whether they should be involved in individual research projects have also been discussed. It has been suggested that research should be conducted by a team other than the clinical team responsible for care. In a research project in the States, where people were performing rapid autopsies on the brains of patients suffering from Alzheimer's disease, it had been suggested that the terminal care of those patients had been affected by the research team's enthusiasm for acquiring rapid autopsies.

Finally, to conclude, I think it is vitally important that the professionals, the Mental Health Act Commission, the Law Commission and others concerned with incompetent subjects and those concerned with the care of mentally ill people should unite to produce safeguards and guidelines. We must do it together in order to create a unified policy about the way we are protecting the rights of mentally disordered patients.

CONSENT TO TREATMENT AND PART IV OF THE MENTAL HEALTH ACT

Dr M Harper
Mental Health Act Commissioner
Senior Lecturer and Honorary Consultant Psychiatrist
University of Wales College of Medicine

INTRODUCTION

Part IV of the Act involves the responsibilities of Second Opinion Doctors appointed by the Commission. Section 58 of the Act concerns treatment for detained patients which can only be given either after a certificate is signed by the Responsible Medical Officer (RMO) that the patient consents or after a second opinion from an appointed doctor certifies that it should be given. This Section applies to the administration of ECT to a detained patient and to drug treatment after three months. These measures involve nearly every practising psychiatrist, whereas the provisions of Section 57 (concerning psychosurgery and the surgical implantation of hormones to suppress the male sexual drive) affect only a minority of patients, but have generated considerable and continuing controversy. This is especially because they apply to consenting informal patients as well as to detained patients.

THE AUTHORITY OF THE CONSULTANT

For voluntary and detained patients prior to 1959 and for detained patients under the 1959 Act the decision of the consultant was regarded as sufficient authority for the administration of treatment, and this was given compulsorily if necessary. This practice included patients admitted for 28 days' observation under Section 25 as well as those held under emergency procedures such as Section 29 and regarded informal patients under Section 30. Indeed, it did not occur to most of us that detention without treatment was either a feasible or a morally justifiable option.

This assumption of authority included the incapable patient. Many of the patients admitted informally since 1959 have been incapable of giving valid consent, usually because of organic dementia, but until recently this was no impediment to their receiving active nursing care and necessary treatment. When a general anaesthetic was required for surgery unrelated to the mental illness it was quite usual for the consultant or a responsible relative to sign the consent form on the patient's behalf, even though it is now understood that this is not legally valid.

In psychiatry, signing consent on behalf of an incapable informal patient has probably all but ceased, leaving staff and the patient in a legal limbo; but this practice is still commonplace in the general surgical wards.

The discussions preceding the 1959 Act as summarised by the Royal Commission (on the Law Relating to Mental Illness and Mental Deficiency[1]) do not question the assumptions concerning compulsory treatment which I have described as standard practice up to 1983.

The main conclusions in the report of the Royal Commission contain this statement (para. 33, p. 9): 'Every effort should be made to persuade patients and their relatives to agree to care without compulsion. But if such efforts fail, doctors and others should not be too hesitant to use the compulsory powers which the law provides, when this seems the only way of giving the patient treatment or training which he badly needs or when such powers are necessary for the protection of others.'

Anxiety was expressed however about the legal validity of compulsory treatment for patients admitted for observation. It was also suggested that the authority to treat patients detained under Section 26 should be defined and made explicit. This issue was particularly raised by the legal advice given to COHSE in 1977, which was that the 1959 Act could not be taken to confer on staff any right to impose treatment. That is, the anxieties were about the risks to staff rather than the risks to patients.

With respect to the treatment of mentally abnormal offenders, the Butler report[2] (para. 3.53, p. 48) of 1975 cited the National Council of Civil Liberties who felt '. . . that to confer on doctors unqualified powers of treatment without consent was unsafe insofar as doctors might, even with the best intentions, abuse this privileged position in their enthusiasm to treat a disorder'.

THE LIMITATIONS IMPOSED BY LAW

The direct and indirect implications of the new consent provisions in Section IV of the Act are still being explored, as the recent judgement on the W. case indicates.* The Act states that compulsory treatment can only be given for mental disorder and there is still no clear guidance on consent for treatment not related to mental disorder for an incompetent patient. This remains a no man's land between the duty of care and the law of battery.

The uncompromisingly dualistic concepts entrenched in the Act can be illustrated by the Commission's Draft Code of Practice[3] which states, (4.9.14) 'If the proposed treatment for a "refusing" patient is for a physical condition which is neither causing nor contributing to the mental disorder, (even if it is itself caused by, or contributed to by, the mental disorder), the following principles of good practice should be observed: No treatment can be given under the Mental Health Act because the treatment is not "for" mental disorder.'

The provisions of Section 57 of the Mental Health Act include informal patients suffering from mental illness who are not necessarily in hospital or liable to be detained and who are capable of giving valid consent. This intrusion

*This concerned the administration to an informal patient of gorserelin—a potent anti-androgenic hormone analogue given by depot injection to suppress male sex drive.

7

into the doctor/patient relationship arouses strongly negative feelings in most practising clinicians. It not only implies a lack of confidence in the profession but it also tends to restigmatise the psychiatrically ill, negating the positive features of the 1959 Act.

The increasingly adversarial nature of hearings before the Mental Health Review Tribunals, the legal impediments to the treatment in the community of patients with a known liability to relapse without such treatment, who then require compulsory readmission, and the anti-psychiatry attitudes which these difficulties seem to represent may well be driving doctors into a more defensive position.

The restrictions now imposed on the exercise of professional judgement are difficult to justify in objective terms and seem a poor reward from the community for the positive advances in treatment which have been won with so much difficulty over the last three decades.

CONSENT OR A SECOND OPINION

While the provisions of Section 57 relating to psychosurgery and the implantation of sex hormones are of considerable and continuing significance in principle and practice, it is Section 58 which intrudes into every day clinical work within the hospital setting. The consent procedures for the administration of ECT to detained patients and for drug treatment after three months represent the interface between the profession and the Mental Health Act Commission on a day to day basis.

There is much scope for misunderstanding. Even after six years of the Act it is not always realised by clinicians that ECT to a detained patient who is capable of consenting and who signs the ECT consent form also requires the formal certification by the RMO on Form 38, under Section 58(3) (a) of the Act, that the patient is capable of giving consent, understands the nature, purpose and likely effect of the treatment and consents to it.

There are no generally accepted clinical tests for determining this consent which will clearly vary from patient to patient and I think it would be unhelpful to attempt to specify criteria for this certification too closely. Consent to a treatment widely if erroneously regarded as frightening and hazardous should certainly not depend upon the patient's ability to recall a dissertation on ECT or on the interpretation of some standard written account. While consent must be informed and sustained to be valid, it must also take due note of the patient's disturbed mental state, of the balance of risks involved and of the alternatives available.

A detained patient who has consented to ECT may withdraw consent, but such a withdrawal of consent should be more than the expression of doubt and anxiety which many of us would feel when facing treatment. Many patients immediately prior to ECT express their fears and need the support and reassurance of the nursing staff before accepting it. There is clearly a difficult line to be drawn between a patient who is persuaded to maintain his expression of consent in spite of doubts and fears and the patient who changes his mind and withdraws consent at the least minute and whose wishes have to be respected. It is presumably to avoid such difficulties that more and more requests for second opinions are being sought for detained patients prescribed ECT.

THE 'SECOND OPINION'

In the consultation document[4] prior to the 1983 Act and in the subsequent White Paper[5] the criteria described in the Butler report[2] for treatments which are hazardous and irreversible are recapitulated and it is recommended that consent for such treatment should be subject to approval by a multidisciplinary panel constituted on an area basis. This was modified by the Act into the confirmation of treatment plan by the second opinion doctor appointed by the Commission.

Here it should be noted that the appointed doctor who visits to assess the patient awaiting ECT, psychosurgery, the implantation of hormones to reduce sexual drive or drugs after three months, is not providing a second opinion in the usual sense of that term.

In the traditional second opinion, the doctor is invited by the consultant, shares responsibility for diagnosis and treatment and is expected to re-examine the patient, to suggest new lines of investigation or treatment where these are indicated and to support the responsible doctor.

The SOAD is appointed by the Commission with a limited function. It is to evaluate the patient's capacity to consent and to approve or disapprove a programme of treatment presented by the RMO.

This will include a consideration of diagnosis, but only so far as it relates to the necessity and legal validity of the detention. It is not the statutory function of the appointed doctor to suggest alternative treatment, but in practice if there is some doubt about the course of action being proposed by the RMO then a new treatment programme may be jointly agreed. The judgement in the W. case indicates that this is a legitimate expectation, without which there can be 'procedural unfairness'.

It has been pointed out before that, if the appointed doctor vetoes the treatment plan, this still leaves the RMO with the responsibility for the management of the patient and there is no statutory machinery for an appeal or an alternative opinion from the Commission, even if a judicial review is remotely available.

The appointed doctor is required to consult a nurse and 'an other person involved in the patient's treatment who is neither a nurse nor a doctor'. The difficulties which this attempt to foster consensus management and multidisciplinary team work by statute has engendered will be familiar to all clinicians and is a vivid illustration of the gap in understanding between our legislators in Parliament assembled and clinical reality. Most often the patients requiring ECT are elderly depressives, refusing fluid and nourishment and requiring considerable nursing care. Here statute law is clearly out of touch with the ward situation. Very often there is no 'other' involved in the

9

care, apart from the social worker making the application, and it has been suggested that the ASW is not 'professionally concerned with the patient's treatment'.

The draft judicial review *ex parte* W. states that, 'It is not entirely clear why it is appropriate for non-medically qualified people to be consulted on the desirability of medical treatment, having regard to the likelihood of it alleviating the patient's condition or preventing its deterioration.' Many consultants would share that view.

However, without consultation with the nurse and 'the other', the certificate cannot be issued, so various *ad hoc* arrangements have to be made to consult with staff whose knowledge of the patient and experience of ECT may be questionable.

URGENT AND NECESSARY TREATMENT

It is recognised in the Act that urgent treatment may need to be given without securing consent and Section 62 allows for such treatment. This section states that the consent provisions are not applicable if the treatment is immediately necessary to save the patient's life, to prevent a serious deterioration, to alleviate serious suffering or to prevent behaviour which is violent or a danger to the patient or others. Treatment which is irreversible cannot be given under this Section except to save the patient's life, and hazardous treatment cannot be given to alleviate suffering or prevent danger.

It should be noted that the short term sections of the Act are expressly excluded from the consent provisions of Part IV and therefore Section 62 cannot be applied. In particular, treatment to a patient admitted under Section 4 or detained under Section 5.2 is not covered by the provisions of Section 62. Here Common Law must be relied upon.

Section 62 is used for both drugs and ECT, though it has been suggested that only the first application of ECT in a course of treatment should usually be administered to a patient unable to give consent, without the approval of an appointed doctor under the provisions of Section 58. However, the Commission administration, who arrange the visit of the SOAD, is not available out of normal office hours, at weekends or over bank holidays, and there is no emergency rota of appointed doctors. Consultants have expressed considerable frustration over the total absence of Commission guidance and the appointed doctor arrangements when their urgent calls to the Commission are met only by an answering machine.

If a second opinion is necessary for the routine administration of ECT to a patient unable to give consent, why is this procedure not available in the more demanding situation of emergency treatment, when more than one application of ECT may be necessary to save the life of a psychotically depressed patient before the formal procedures of the Act can be instituted? The patient is surely more at risk out of hours and at times of staff shortage than when the wards are fully staffed and the administrative machinery of the hospital is working normally.

I take these anomalies to indicate that the consent provisions under Section 58 and Section 62 are more concerned with safeguards to reassure the general public about compulsory treatment than with the immediate protection of the vulnerable patient. This remains, as it must, with the profession.

A certain disenchantment with the system is also apparent when the medical profession considers the details of the certification of treatment. What is a course of ECT? Should this be 12 treatments or as many treatments as it takes? The Commission requires its appointed doctors to ensure that the treatment plan for ECT is specific rather than open ended—on the basis that the patient has to be presented with a proposition of finite proportions before either giving or refusing consent. Here there has been some misunderstanding. The appointed doctor is not required to impose an arbitrary limit on the treatment programme. However, unusually extensive and prolonged treatment is likely to be subject to special scrutiny and the indications justified. A course of treatment will usually be for up to twelve treatments, but more can be agreed if this is necessary, especially when this is indicated by the patient's previous response to treatment.

It might be thought that consent relating to a plan of drug treatment would be more straightforward. This aspect of the legislation is an uneasy compromise between those who were against any drug treatment being imposed on a patient and those who were prepared to allow the RMO to continue to prescribe unhindered. The three months is not dated from the time of admission under compulsion, but from the time during a continuous period of detention when medication was first prescribed—not a date which can be easily identified. It was assumed that by three months the patient's treatment would have stabilised. It was suggested to the Standing Committee[6] that, 'The three months gives time for the psychiatrist to consider a treatment programme which suits the patient. Three months seems to fit in best with both clinical experience and clinical practice. It is long enough to allow a proper evaluation and assessment of what, if any, long term treatment may be needed. It is also short enough to ensure the patient's consent or a second opinion is obtained before a long term course of drug treatment gets too far ahead'.

In practice many patients who are still detained and not consenting after three months of drug treatment either have a multitude of problems and complications or lack the capacity to consent. Their treatment needs to be continually reviewed and modified in the light of the clinical situation and new approaches tried to control the psychosis and attempt rehabilitation.

THE TREATMENT PLAN

The Commission has recommended to its appointed doctors that the treatment plan should describe the treatment in broad terms, identifying the medication by the categories within the National Formulary rather than by specific drug, giving the route of administration and doses in terms of a dose range to allow for flexibility. Otherwise a change from flupenthixol decanoate to haloperidol decanoate or every change of dosage requires the recertification of consent or an additional visit by the appointed doctor. Unfortunately, this advice has not yet been effectively circulated to RMOs, many of whom prefer to interpret the statute by indicating the broad class of drug—antidepressants or major tranquillisers, without specifying the route or the dose. Others are content to complete the forms by certifying 'drugs for mental illness' in spite of the guidance included in the DDL of 84(4). Whatever is written on the form, the essential matter is obtaining valid consent by the consultant. The form merely reflects and records this process which must depend upon the skills, judgement and ethics of the profession.

Many clinicians would be reluctant to unsettle an anxious or partially controlled but compliant psychotic patient by a recital of all the hazards theoretically associated with the medication the patient had been taking for three months—and yet good practice dictates that patients should be informed and continuously involved in their treatment as far as possible, even when insight is limited and compliance absent or uncertain.

CONCLUSIONS

Some of the difficulties of implementing the consent provisions of Section 58 have been outlined and attention drawn to the negative attitudes which this part of the Act still engenders. Considering the large numbers of second opinions, (at least 3000 a year) the very considerable difficulties which patients needing a second opinion generally present and the limited resources available within the hospitals and within the Commission it is remarkable that the implementation of the compulsory second opinion provision has gone as smoothly as it has.

Statute law, the Code of Practice, the periodic visits of the Mental Health Act Commission, the provision of independent doctors to review consent and to provide a compulsory second opinion all contribute to good practice. But the law and the Commission cannot be everywhere, and the real safeguard lies in the professionalism of the clinical team, particularly on the skill, training, experience, leadership qualities and ethical standards of the responsible medical officer.

The Butler report expressed this succinctly when discussing the issue of consent in a detained offender patient (para 3.56, p. 49). 'We recognise that in this respect, as in others, the patient is well safeguarded by the professional ethics of the doctors responsible for his treatment.' The report continues, 'For this reason we have rejected any idea of proposing detailed rules for the guidance of doctors, with a view to the protection of patients.'

In this light the consent provisions of the 1983 Act, however cumbersome, should not be seen as driving the profession in an unwelcome direction, but rather as a milestone on the road from paternalism to participation by the patient in his treatment. This has been an accepted element in British psychiatric practice for over half a century.

Although the consent to treatment provisions of Section 58 are a bureaucratic encumbrance, they give formal expression to principles which protect the most vulnerable of our patients and for this reason they should be welcomed.

I wish to make it clear that my paper on the Consent to Treatment provisions of the Mental Health Act consists only of my own views and does not represent or reflect the official position of the Mental Health Act Commission.

REFERENCES

1 Cmnd. 169. Royal Commission on the Law Relating to Mental Illness and Mental Deficiency 1954–1957. HMSO 1957.
2 Cmnd. 6244. Home Office, Department of Health and Social Security. Report of the Committee on Mentally Abnormal Offenders. HMSO 1975.
3 Mental Health Act 1983: Section 118. Draft Code of Practice. Mental Health Division, Department of Health and Social Security. 1985.
4 Department of Health and Social Security. A Review of the Mental Health Act 1959. HMSO 1976.
5 Cmnd. 7320. Department of Health and Social Security, Home Office, Welsh Office, Lord Chancellor's Department. Review of the Mental Health Act 1959. HMSO 1978.
6 Special Standing Committee of the House of Commons, June 29, 1982. In: Mental Health Act Manual (ed Jones R). London: Sweet & Maxwell, 1985.

DISCUSSION

Audience   Professor Murphy, we have all had experience of trying to get adequate legal opinions in 'grey areas'. As you say, the first recourse should be perhaps to the district or regional solicitor. We all know how unsatisfactory that is. You then suggested a privately obtained opinion might be preferable. I would like you to clarify why that should be a more satisfactory source of legal advice than that given by the Mental Health Act Commission, whose legal members are in daily contact with the problems and interpretation of the Act?

Professor Murphy   I share your anxieties and I have only recently been converted to this way of thinking. The Commission has 13 legal members and I think will offer 13 different legal opinions on any one question. The major concern is that a brief telephone call or letter often hides a very complex issue and every case is quite individual. I agree that there are some common questions that come to the Commission, and that is why it has been decided to compile a handbook which all commissioners can use, giving advice on common legal questions. However, the cases that develop are unique and therefore individuals ought to seek advice from their own legal adviser. The Commission can only offer an opinion.

Dr Bradley   The Medical Protection Society receives more requests for advice from psychiatrists than any other professional group.

Audience   Dr Harper, the three months period of treatment starts from the date of prescription. Does that mean that if the prescription antedated the Section that it starts before that Section?

Dr Harper   The three months starts once the patient is detained. If the patient is in hospital and is then detained, it would date from the start of detention, but if the patient is admitted and under detention and is not treated for three weeks, then the three months period starts from the date when medication is administered. The legislators did not realise how difficult it was going to be to work out. It is not a date that easily comes to mind.

Audience   Professor Murphy, elderly, demented, confused patients are admitted to hospital and classified as 'voluntary patients'. In fact, often they cannot give an opinion or consent to admission or treatment. Is this ethical to detain someone who does not actually ask to leave, but at the same time cannot really voice any sort of informed consent?

Dr Murphy   The Commission is very concerned about these individuals. You are talking about informal patients who are *de facto* detained for whatever reason. There are no hard and fast rules about how to treat those patients, except what we have already established in terms of the 'balancing act'. In fact,

14

at the moment, I am more concerned as I go round hospitals that there are nurses, and therapists particularly, who appear to be frightened to implement their duty of care because they are concerned that they will be interfering with the rights of these individuals, and there the door is left unlocked exposing the patients to more risk than if they were actually detained behind doors. It is a very good example of where we do need some guidance. The Commission will be asking the Secretary of State in its review, about *de facto* detained elderly patients and mentally handicapped patients in registered nursing homes and hospitals.

Audience   Dr Harper, you said that the Commission is being requested about 3000 times a year to arrange a second opinion; in what number of cases has the Commission doctor disagreed with the recommendation of the other?

Dr Harper   I think it is a very small proportion; (actually 4–6%) doctors tend to agree on treatment and if they do disagree they often will find a compromise.

Audience   I think such a number is the crux of the matter. There is a basic implication that some doctors act immorally, unethically or illegally. It is about time that this kind of presumption was countered.

Dr Harper   I understand those feelings, but we must see this as a public relations exercise and as a safeguard imposed by statute law; we must embrace and endorse it and make it work.

POLICY RESPONSE TO CHANGING CLINICAL TRENDS

Dr John Shanks
Principal Medical Officer
Department of Health
(*delivered on behalf of Dr John Reed*)

INTRODUCTION

The basis of current Government policy for mental health services is the two White Papers 'Better Services for the Mentally Handicapped' (1971) and 'Better Services for the Mentally Ill' (1975).

These documents signalled the first major change in mental health policy since the passing of the first Asylum Act in 1808. However, the pattern of treatment which the White Papers describe, namely one involving less in-patient care and greater use of alternative, less institutional forms of care had been developing long before the 1970's, since at least the time of the 1930 Mental Treatment Act, which made voluntary admission possible. Then, as now, policy development was essentially evolutionary not revolutionary.

In 1981 'Care in Action' identified three main tasks for health authorities in developing services for mentally ill people. These are:

1. To create a local comprehensive mental illness service in each District, reducing the catchment area of multi-district mental illness hospitals to their own district.
2. To create a psychogeriatric service in each health district.
3. To arrange for the closure of those mental illness hospitals which are not well placed for the districts which they serve and which are already near the end of their useful life.

It is by no means a matter of chance that development of local services is mentioned before closure of hospitals. Closure of hospitals is not now, and has never been, a primary aim of policy. The fall in the resident population of mental illness hospitals started long before publication of present policies which, indeed, were formulated following consideration of the existing statistical trends and of current mental illness practice. As the population of mental illness hospitals falls because of better treatment and through the death of those elderly patients who have spent very long times in hospital, so it may become sensible to close a hospital to ensure the best use of resources. But Ministers are adamant that no hospital should close until satisfactory alternative services have been provided.

If that is the policy, then are we sure that it is working across the country as we would want it to? We need in the Department to have a clear picture of what is going on at a local level. In the next year or so we will be looking closely at what services there are on the ground, particularly from the point of view of the patient. We need to know more about what is available to patients and their families when they seek help in each region in the country. On the basis of this work, Ministers will consider whether there are any steps that it is right and practical to take to improve the care of mentally ill people. Policy is not static. It developed as a reflection of clinical practice and it must continue to take note of and respond to areas of current anxiety. I would like to discuss briefly a few areas of particular concern.

LONG-TERM MENTAL ILLNESS

The Government, in responding to the Social Services Select Committee Report on Community Care in 1985, agreed with the Committee that the real measure of success of a service was not whether it meets adequately the needs of those who least require the service, but whether it meets well the needs of those who most require it. One group of people most needing the service are those who suffer long-term and serious disability because of mental illness.

The advent of the neuroleptic drugs and other improvements in treatment has meant that many people who would previously have spent months or years in hospital are now fit to be discharged, after a relatively brief in-patient stay.

However many are likely to need continuing care. Services face a major challenge to ensure that such patients, when in the community, receive the continuing care they require with as much certainty and with as regular reassessment of their needs as would have been available to them if they had remained in hospital. It is clear from many accounts, both scientific and in the media, that this does not always occur. Reports showing that up to 50% of destitute, homeless people are suffering from serious mental disorder and research showing an unacceptably high number of mentally ill people in the prison system indicate a serious problem. What is the source of the problem? Often these problems are attributed to a shortage of beds for mentally ill people and the consequences of hospital run-downs and closures. However, you will find that, at the end of 1986, there were, in England, some 10 000 empty, staffed mental illness beds and also some 8000 vacant day hospital places. Faced with statistics such as these it is hard to avoid the conclusion that part of the problem is one of effective distribution of resources rather than of a shortage of beds or day hospital places. Moreover, in listening to the accounts of destitute, homeless, mentally ill people and those in prison, although some may report having been discharged to unsuitable accommodation such as a doss-house, a much commoner story is that they have been discharged to quite suitable accommodation and care but then later lost touch with the services, moved and 'fell out from care' into destitution or the criminal justice system. Failure of continuity of community care appears as a common feature behind many of the cases of which we hear.

Recognising that there are difficulties in ensuring continuity of care in the community the Department of Health has, over recent years, commissioned research into this problem in Salford, Southampton and Hackney. Ministers have received reports of these and other projects. With the intention of

17

improving continuity of care in the community the current NHS Planning Guidelines (HC(88)43) require each health authority as a new service objective to establish by 1991 'care programmes' for those people chronically disabled by mental illness who are living mainly in the community. As a policy aim each health authority is also required to identify a consultant with special responsibility for continuing care and rehabilitation. The Department will be publishing further guidance on this subject dealing with case management, community review and the use of computerised 'at risk' registers in the near future.

Asylum, in the sense of a safe refuge, is a necessary part of any comprehensive service, but this refuge can be provided in many settings beside an institutional one. Not all those who need a refuge need the same type of refuge. A range of options is required to provide asylum both in the community—through different types of supported accommodation—and through long-term in-patient care. The need for some long-term, in-patient care for younger mentally ill people has been envisaged in policy documents since 1975 when hospital hostels were first mentioned. The Department has over the years funded research into ways in which long-term in-patient care can be offered to highly dependent patients in ways that avoid some of the problems of conventional long-stay wards. Because we considered this research on 'hospital hostels' so important we have in the last year completed five seminars up and down the country publicising the results. A book summarising the findings will be published shortly.

SPECIAL HOSPITALS

Some mentally disordered people need treatment in conditions of such high levels of security that this can only be met in the 'Special Hospitals' established specifically for that purpose under the NHS Act 1977. There are at present some 1725 beds in the four special hospitals managed directly by the Department of Health. The appropriateness of this arrangement has, in recent years, been subject to increasing debate and critical scrutiny—within Government Departments, within the health care professions, by academics and by groups representing the interests of patients in particular and of the public in general. Over the last year or so the management arrangements for the special hospitals have come under review. Ministers have decided to establish a central Special Hospital Service Authority responsible for the management of the national special hospital service and the introduction of general management within these hospitals. The operation of the new arrangements will be kept under review to assess the results of the changes.

At a clinical level published research done at Broadmoor has suggested that many of the patients there no longer require the very high levels of security offered by special hospital care. To examine this further, the Department of Health is commissioning research from Professor Gunn at the Institute of Psychiatry to establish the treatment and security needs of patients in all the Special Hospitals. We hope to have this information available within two years. This, coupled with comparable research by Professor Gunn into the mental health needs of the prison population and an appraisal of what is available within the NHS–both in Regional Secure Units and elsewhere will give us a sound basis for assessment of the need for treatment facilities offering varying degrees of security. These will range from the Special Hospital at one extreme to intensive care units or beds in ordinary hospitals or DGH units at the other.

MENTAL HANDICAP

The aim of policy is to develop a comprehensive range of co-ordinated health and social services for mentally handicapped people and their families with a major shift from institutional care to a range of local care facilities according to individual needs. As a consequence, the run down of large mental handicap hospitals will continue. Social service departments will play an increasingly important role but there will continue to be a need for some specialised residential health care.

It is in this latter area that we are concerned that some authorities appear to be having difficulties in meeting the needs of those relatively few adult mentally handicapped people who show severely disturbed behaviour. Over the last year or so a working group—led by Department of Health officials—has been looking at the ways in which different authorities have successfully met their special needs. The Department of Health will very shortly publish a discussion paper setting out the results of this enquiry.

PRIMARY CARE

I am anxious that we should not confine our attention to hospital services because we know that only a small proportion of people with significant mental disorder get referred to the specialist secondary care services. Of 230 people attending their GP with significant psychological symptoms only 17 will be referred to psychiatrists and only 6 admitted to hospital.

There is now good evidence that better detection and treatment by the primary care team particularly of affective disorder will lead to improved clinical outcomes and lessened burden on patients and their families.

An area of great importance is the relationship between primary and secondary mental health care. This becomes increasingly important as the secondary care teams move away from their hospital base and into the community which they serve. On a day to day basis, primary and secondary care workers need to know clearly who is responsible for what aspect of a patient's care, who is the key worker to whom the patient relates, who the case manager and who the responsible consultant. There is an increasing need for accurate and up to date communication between the members of the primary and secondary care teams so that decisions are informed by the latest events, in order that prompt action may avert deterioration, and avoid patients 'falling through the net'.

As more of the secondary care staff move into the community, there is concern that resources which were previously devoted to major psychiatric morbidity (the severe psychoses) will become diverted in part to the care of minor psychiatric morbidity e.g. neurotic reactions and adjustment disorders. Of course both ends of the spectrum require early detection, accurate assessment and effective treatment. The manner in which the secondary and primary care services are deployed will be crucial in determining whether an effective service is delivered. We need to establish cost effective ways of detecting and treating minor psychiatric morbidity by primary care teams so that the secondary care teams, continue to focus mainly on the severely mentally ill. Furthermore, secondary care teams should develop an important role in educating and supporting primary care teams in their increasing involvement in the care of mental illness, and in preventive initiatives.

COMMUNITY CARE

Both for mentally ill people and for mentally handicapped people community care is as essential an element of a comprehensive range of local services as is hospital care. Both need to be provided in balanced proportion. Over-provision of in-patient facilities cannot compensate for under provision of community care any more than community care can operate effectively without supporting hospital services.

The Audit Commission in their valuable document 'Making a reality of Community Care' highlighted many of the difficulties inherent in the organisation of community services. Following this, Ministers asked Sir Roy Griffiths to undertake an overview of the way in which public funds are used to support community care policy and to suggest options for ways to improve the effective use of these funds. His report 'Community Care: Agenda for Action' was delivered to Secretary of State in February 1988. Since then detailed consideration has been given to the report and to formulating a response and this will be published at the earliest opportunity. A carefully considered response is vital; it is more important to get it right than to get a response out rapidly.

CONCLUSION

The changes which the mental health services are going through are evolutionary but they are also profound. A locally based service with a high element of community care is very different to an institutionally-based service. Different skills and attitudes are needed, relationships are changed both between the various professions and between the professions, patients and their families.

We need to ask ourselves some questions. Do we have a too laissez-faire attitude in allowing patients to drop out of care in the community when we would not allow a patient with similar disabilities to drop out from care in hospital? Perhaps a greater sense of continuing responsibility for patients who have been discharged is needed.

Are we too rigid about catchment areas? Sometimes patients who are unfortunate enough to end up in prision or destitute are viewed as someone else's problem both by the service from which they came and by the catchment area in which they now find themselves.

Do we take enough notice of the views of our patients as consumers? Most mentally ill destitute people have been our patients in the past but, although seriously ill, are notably reluctant to seek our help again—do we ask ourselves why?

The new practice of psychiatry and the provision of local services has been a great benefit to the great majority of patients but there are undoubtedly some areas where problems exist. The challenge is to solve these within the framework of present policy to which Ministers remain firmly committed. *Crown copyright 1989.*

DISCUSSION

Audience I believe that the Poor Laws were introduced originally when parishes expected vagrants and the psychiatrically disturbed to be unpopular to move them to other parishes because they were an encumbrance in any feudal system which existed. Do you have views on how Kenneth Clarke proposes these groups should be dealt with in his new National Health Service?

Dr Shanks We are talking about the implications of the NHS review in the White Paper for Mental Illness services, and that is my area of interest. This question is one we are considering and discussing with the profession; it is clear that the White Paper deliberately leaves many areas to be worked out by agreement at the local level, particularly with regard to mental illness. It should be reassuring to note that mental illness services are mentioned among the 'core services' to which every district is likely to require guaranteed local access. The forthcoming White Paper on Community Care will spell out arrangements in more detail.

The problem of homeless mentally ill people is one of which we are well aware. The problem here may be a failure of a continuity of care; that it is easy to lose touch with people as the community based service develops. We shall have to develop methods of keeping in contact with people when they are no longer in hospital. There are good examples of practice here. There are several areas in the country where computerised registers are running that flag up patients who do not keep in contact with the professionals. It is then possible to go out and seek them and indulge in assertive case finding, and I believe that and similar things may lead to ways in which we can actually continue to provide an effective service in the new look NHS.

Audience Are the pyschiatric services, particulary those for the elderly mentally ill, to remain a priority service, and will finance for them be secured?

21

Dr Shanks   Yes, the mental illness services still have that priority, especially for the elderly. The mental illness services have been identified as being likely core services in the White Paper following the NHS review. As far as funds are concerned, measures are already in existence to safeguard and increase these and also to 'ring-fence' others as they become available, for example, those funds released by the selling of mental hospital land. The Department has recently strengthened the Land Transaction regulations further to make sure that those circumstances which Health Authorities might claim as being exceptional are scrutinised and agreed by us before funds are moved.

Audience   You have not mentioned the role of the home carer. These people are really informal primary care team members. What priority and importance is the Department giving to these carers? If ignored the NHS will come to its knees.

Dr Shanks   I agree absolutely. The Department is well aware that the service could not function without the goodwill and skill of relatives who look after the majority of psychiatric morbidity. A number of research projects are being funded at the moment to look at ways in which the Department can support that activity.

Audience   You have explained your policy using statistics which give the number of vacant mental health beds. We have also heard that the Department by its own admission is saying that is it not sufficiently close to the ground to know what provisions and developments are needed. Considering the pace of change of any switchover from one type of provision to another, how can you be sure that your statistics will not misguide you, for example, the number of vacancies? What safeguards have you built into the change in case you are wrong?

Dr Shanks   The defects have been identified; we do not have sufficiently accurate local information and we propose to remedy it. A rolling programme of closer contact with regions and districts has been mounted so that we become better informed and more aware of the consequence of the pace of change. Certainly the Department has been insisting recently on scrutinising more closely any plans to close mental illness hospitals and to make sure that ministers can be absolutely sure that satisfactory community services are there first before any hospital ceases to provide that service. It is terribly important and we are emphasising this even more than we did in the past.

Audience   One of the biggest causes of breaks in the continuity of care is a lapse of treatment. Could you let us know the Department's view on receiving proposals for a refurbished Community Treatment Order?

Dr Shanks   The Department is in the position of promoting and observing a debate by the professions. There is not yet a consensus among the doctors and other professionals who would be involved in such an order; whether or not it would be desirable and if so in what form. The Department is working through the Royal College of Psychiatrists and other professional bodies to try and find that consensus. It does not yet exist and there are no current plans to recommend Community Treatment Order.

Audience   I wish to refer to the care of patients who are under 70 years of age in North Derbyshire. The teams are based in the community and the doctor is regarded as an equal member of the team, which also contains a psychologist, community nurse and social worker. The communities are defined by local authority boundaries because of the importance of meshing with the Social Services. Sadly the general practitioner and the primary care teams do not fit into these boundaries but overlap them. It is therefore very difficult to work with the primary care teams. Communications break down and, for example, patients who require Modecate injections are not dealt with by the community nurse in the team, but have to trek to the hospital. There ought to be guidelines for all community teams on who gives the injections and how different teams should be coordinated.

Dr Shanks   That problem concerns one aspect of 'drift' which is something that the Americans have been studying. It is very easy for community services to become distracted and preoccupied in dealing with articulate less severely ill patients who present themselves for care on demand. There is a way forward through the deployment of resources between the primary and secondary care teams. I was interested that you said that your primary care teams tend to refer to you, the secondary care specialist teams, less severe problems. We must develop a way in which the primary care team is enabled to manage themselves those less severe problems, leaving colleagues such as yourself and the specialist team free to devote your resources to the more severely ill, because I do believe that is where those specialist resources are best directed.

CONSENT TO PSYCHIATRIC TREATMENT

Dr Nigel Eastman
Senior Lecturer in Forensic Psychiatry
St George's Hospital Medical School

INTRODUCTION

My credentials for presenting this paper are, as a barrister and practising forensic psychiatrist. The invitation to the Conference includes the phrase: 'If you share an interest in the grey area of legal and medical professional co-operation and occasional conflict . . .'. Many may take issue with the notion of 'occasional conflict' but I would disagree more with the notion of a 'grey area'. In reality, I think that there is more of a black/white interface, based on the fact that law and medicine come from very different philosophical and epistemological traditions. Perhaps the interface only appears to be grey because we often fail to distinguish the boundary where one discipline stops and the other begins. So my aim in this paper is to attempt to elucidate the nature of that boundary, specifically in relation to the law and ethics concerning consent to psychiatric treatment. I shall do so in a general sense, but will include also some recent legal decisions, together with some of the (scant) empirical research which has been published.

RELATIONSHIP BETWEEN LAW AND ETHICS

By way of a preface the general relationship between the law and ethics should be addressed. It is unavoidable in a general sense, but it is particularly unavoidable in the area of consent to treatment.

There is an interrelationship between ethics and the law which operates in both directions. Clearly ethics influences the law. Indeed, in an ideal world you might hope that law amounted to 'applied ethics'; however, if you attended the Strangers' Gallery of the House of Commons and looked into the 'monkey pit' below you might be forgiven for coming to the conclusion that what you are watching was not a considered ethical debate. The latter points clearly to the fact that there are other influences on our law making, these being political, sociological, religious and cultural for example. The relationship operates in the opposite direction as well; law can influence ethics. If you are raised in a country where it is legal to cut off somebody's hand if they steal then clearly your personal ethical structures may be somewhat different from those which would derive from living in a country where thieves are sometimes given probation orders. It is perhaps not always recognised how important our legal structure is in determining how we think ethically. Of course, there are many other factors that determine ethical thinking apart from the law; again, these are religious, cultural, sociological and, perhaps in a true behavioural sense, we also 'learn' ethics.

There may be coherence between the law and ethics, but there is no necessary coherence between the two. As an example, if you are in a situation where you think it to be ethically right to treat a patient but the Mental Health Act 1983[1] determines that you cannot do so then you will be acutely aware of that lack of coherence. Finally, as regards the general relationship, essentially ethics fills legal 'gaps' arising because the law is 'silent' on many matters. There is a legal fiction that the law actually exists in relation to any situation and that by going to court it can be identified. Hence the judge may say, 'The law is . . .', thereby implying it existed in the ether and he has simply observed it. Of course, he has just 'made it up'. But, in the absence of going to court to find out what the law is, the citizen is left only with legal opinion as to what the law might be and, ultimately, his own ethical structure.

ETHICAL AND LEGAL BASES OF CONSENT

Let me turn specifically to consent, and both the ethical and legal bases for its requirement.

Ethicists postulate different bases for the requirement of consent, but the 'front runner' is undoubtedly the principle of autonomy. Even a lawyer may enunciate clearly the primary ethical root of the requirement of consent. For instance, Michael Sherrard QC, when giving legal opinion to the BMA Council as regards HIV testing without consent, said 'It is a fundamental principle that a human being has the right to determine what should be done with his or her own body'.[2] Similarly, the World Medical Association Declaration of Helsinki 1964, at greater length and with qualifications, states 'If at all possible, consistent with patient psychology, the doctor should obtain the patient's freely given consent after the patient has been given a full explanation'.[3]

Now let us consider the legal translation of this ethical principle, autonomy. There are, in fact, essentially two such translations. The 'pure' translation is contained within the legal notion of battery. If I touch somebody, where they do not say I can do so, then that is a battery. That legal concept arises out of the autonomy principle in a rather direct fashion; the coherence of ethics and law in Michael Sherrard's own definition makes this clear.

But there is another translation of the principle of autonomy and that is in terms of the legal notion of negligence. A doctor can be negligent not only in practical procedures but also through not giving the patient enough information about those practical procedures, such that the patient does not have enough information to operate his autonomy. It is, therefore, in the sense of autonomy operation that I mean that negligence is the translation into law of the principle of autonomy. There is another important and apparently contradictory aspect of negligence. The courts might consider you to be negligent not to override a patient refusing treatment. In that case the court would have considered that there was a duty of care to that patient.

Clinicians live every day therefore in constant tension, both ethical and legal, between two sets of principles, both in ethical terms and their legal translation. In ethical terms the principle of autonomy is set against the principle of paternalism; the legal translation of these two is the consent requirement (which relates to autonomy) and duty of care (which relates to paternalism).

ETHICAL AND LEGAL DEFINITION OF CONSENT

Let us consider the ethical definition of consent in broad terms. First, reconsider the WMA Helsinki Declaration, 'If at all possible, consistent with patient psychology, the doctor should obtain the patient's freely given consent after the patient has received a full explanation'. Extracting out the 4 main elements of this definition, they are:

(1) 'consistent with patient psychology', which is to do with patient's competence;
(2) 'freely given' of course means voluntariness;
(3) 'consent' means a decision (in agreement); and finally,
(4) 'after a full explanation' implies that information has been given. There has been published an 'ethical model' (which is actually called by its authors a 'legal model') of consent[4] which essentially incorporates exactly these five elements of the WMA definition.

$$Cp + I \rightarrow U$$
$$U + V \rightarrow D$$

This model requires a competent patient (Cp), who is given information (I) such that the result is the patient understanding the treatment information (U). If there is an 'understanding patient' and a voluntary situation between doctor and the patient (V) and, further, that results in a 'positive' decision by the patient (D), then valid consent exists. If even one element is missing then it does not.

It is important to state that there is a distinction between the fact of an element and evidence as to the fact of an element. Take decision as an example. If it is clear that there is a signed consent form for ECT but that there is also evidence that, the next day, the patient was crawling off the table as attempts were made to pin him down, it will be to little effect to say in court, 'but there was a consent form'. Hence, there is such a distinction between the fact of consent, here the fact of a 'positive' decision, and evidence as to the fact of the decision.

Each of these elements can be considered as conceptually distinct, both ethically and also legally. However, it is, mathematically, rather an odd model because all of the variables are highly interrelated and correlated with each other. For example, considering competence, that 'construct' is related to each of the other variables. Understanding is the empirical correlate of the philosophical notion of competence. Information is related to competence because it sets the threshold of competence; that is, the quality and amount of information you are required to receive determines how mentally competent you have to be to receive it. Similarly, you can fail to make a decision because you are incompetent, as in somebody who is pathologically ambivalent. Finally, voluntariness is partially 'defined' by competence in that the voluntariness of a response of someone who is, for example, very suggestible may be affected by that suggestibility. Competence is, therefore, central to the whole notion of consent, even if the latter general construct can be analysed in terms of its component elements.

Let us now consider separately each element of consent, both ethically and legally.

(1) Information

Essentially here there are two issues. Firstly, what is the required standard of information? Secondly, what are the required types of information?

The standard of information can be either an autonomy ('patient based') standard or a duty of care ('profession based') standard. The seminal legal case in this country is Bolam v Friern Hospital, in which it was determined that the standard that applied was that of 'ordinary professional practice in that particular medical situation', and not 'what was needed by the patient to operate his autonomy'.[5] In the well known and more recent case of Sidaway v Bethlem Royal and Maudsley Hospitals that principle was essentially upheld but 'with strings attached'. The court said that, 'if professional standards in a particular situation are not high enough to satisfy the basic needs of patient autonomy, then the courts reserve the right to say that and to determine, therefore, that you have not in those circumstances achieved valid legal consent'.[6]

The other aspect of the information element is that of the required types of information. This is not clearly delineated legally anywhere. By implication from the Mental Health Act 1983 (from the definition of the mental capacity to consent to treatment) it seems that one is required to give a patient information about the nature, the purpose and likely effects of the treatment. By contrast, a more comprehensive requirement might include having also to tell the patient about the alternative treatments they might have or about 'no treatment' as an option.

(2) Voluntariness

The notion of voluntariness appears to be a simple idea. However, a distinction can be made between three types of 'coercion'. Consider the following three scenarios where a psychiatrist is carrying out a domiciliary visit. In Scenario 1, he sits down with Mrs Jones and says, 'Mrs Jones, if you don't come into hospital then I'm going to section you'; that is overt coercion. In Scenario 2 he says rather 'Hello, Mrs Jones, well here we are again'. (where Mrs Jones knows exactly what that means, because 'last time' she was sectioned when she did not come into hospital voluntarily); she decides that she had better go in because he would section her otherwise. I think that is covert coercion if the doctor had it in his mind to coerce when he says it. In Scenario 3, as the patient pulls the curtain aside and sees the doctor coming up the garden path, she thinks, 'I'd better go in because he is going to section me'. I think that is 'reality coercion', rather than any form of coercion by the doctor. The distinction between 'covert coercion' and 'reality coercion', in particular, may at times be a fine one and may rest upon the form of communication arising from the psychiatrist. Relatedly, a further general distinction is that between 'coercion' and 'persuasion'.

There is one other potential aspect of coercion, that is, 'situation determined' coercion. A man called Freeman sued the Home Office. He was a prisoner and he sued in negligence and battery through saying that he could not, in law, have consented to an injection of Haldol which he received in prison, from a prison medical officer, because he could not have a voluntary relationship with the doctor. The point was based partly on the fact that the doctor was also defined as a 'prison officer'. Louis Blom Cooper QC argued eloquently in the Court of Appeal that there was presumed coercion in that situation.[7] The Court of Appeal did not agree. Relatedly, the case of *Silverman v Mental Health Act Commission* (which was about the use of depot goselerin in a sex offender) was overtly not to do with voluntariness but, rather, was more concerned with the definition of a 'hormone' and of an 'implant' in terms of Section 57 of the Mental Health Act. However, at the time a good deal of concern was expressed, individually by psychiatrists, about the validity of voluntariness where the treatment occurred under a condition of a Probation Order. The crucial distinction there was probably between goselerin as part of the treatment and goselerin as the treatment, in the context of ethical fears that the psychiatrist could, through such 'probation orders with conditions of treatment' act as an arm of the courts.

(3) Decision
This also seems fairly clear; has somebody decided 'yes' or 'no'? However, even so there may, for example, be temporal inconsistency (what I say now may not be what I say tomorrow), or modality inconsistency (where, for example the patient says 'yes' as he walks out of the door).

There is a common misconception, particularly in medical circles, about implied consent; that is, that the boundary of implied consent is wide. Implied consent is, in fact, a very limited notion. There are two varieties of it: (1) the 'reasonable man test', as where the person is unconscious, and (2) the test of the 'attending patient', that is, for example, where the patient comes to the GP's surgery, a certain amount of implied consent can be presumed.

(4) Competence and understanding
Competence and understanding best reflect the notion of the 'grey area' or the 'boundary' between law and psychiatry. They have to be considered together because of their intimate 'constructural' relationship. Competence is so crucial because it relates directly to the legal rules concerning consent; diminished competence triggers, in various ways, exceptions to the requirement of consent. Mental handicap is the paradigm case, as illustrated in Professor Bicknell's paper to this Conference.

Competence can be addressed at two levels, either as an impossibly difficult and (philosophically) 'high level' concept or as a 'lower level' and operational concept. The latter might be called the psychiatric translation of ethical and legal definitions of competence.

What are the legal rules and implied definitions? The common law simply seems to say that the patient has to be capable of 'understanding in broad terms the nature and purpose of the treatment'. The Mental Health Act, which offers the only definition of competence to consent to treatment in statute, says that the patient has to be 'capable of understanding the nature, the purpose and likely effects of the treatment'.[8] Such a broad concept may be of only limited use but, if it is placed clearly in a hierarchy of alternative definitions of competence, then it becomes more valuable through comparison.

Ethically and legally a distinction needs to be made between presumptive incompetence (or competence) and evidential incompetence (or competence). Somebody is presumptively incompetent because, for example, they are only 2 years of age, or presumptively competent because they are 16 years of age and the Family Law Reform Act says they are competent. That is distinct from evidential incompetence (or competence) which requires observation of how the person is functioning. In considering, particularly, mental handicap I would argue that it is necessary to think in evidential terms rather than presumptive terms, for obvious ethical reasons.

There are many alternative ethical (and potentially legal) definitions of competence. Roth *et al.* published a hierarchy from 1 to 6 in the American Journal of Psychiatry in 1977.[9]

(1) evidence of a choice
(2) 'reasonable' outcome of choice
(3) 'rational reasons' based choice
(4) ability to understand treatment information
(5) actual understanding of treatment information
(6) ability to reason on treatment information
    (see e.g. Roth *et al.* Am J Psych 1977)

There are, of course, potentially many different sorts of definitions. Let us now consider, however, each of Roth *et al*'s alternatives in some detail. (1) If the person has only to give evidence of making a choice, they must indicate unambiguously 'yes' or 'no'. That requires nothing concerning the quality of the decision, merely that they just make a choice. (2) If it is required that the choice has a reasonable outcome, that does not address the process of the choice. (3) Thirdly, if it is required that the choice is based on rational reasons, that tries to look at the process through the 'window' of the stated reasons; but that, of course, begs the question 'what is a rational reason?' (which is a subjective notion); also the stated reasons may not be the actual reasons of the person. These latter two definitions are both essentially non-empirical notions whereas, by contrast, evidence of a choice is potentially an empirical notion. The next two stages in the hierarchy, 4 and 5, are intimately related: the ability to understand treatment information and the actual understanding of treatment information. These clearly look at the process of achieving the information, but can actually ignore the outcome of the process; it does not matter

29

if it is an 'irrational' choice, it is the process that matters. The Mental Health Act definition fits into the hierarchy at Stage 4. Stage 5 goes one step further than the Mental Health Act, through requiring, additionally, actual understanding of information. At a higher level of sophistication, Stage 6, it could be argued that the person should be able to reason on the information.

The '3 knows' test is yet another which can be applied. Here the patient is required to know that others think (s)he is ill, that treatments are being offered and that (s)he is required to make a choice.

As regards the general character of incompetence (or competence) this must be considered as a graded concept, and not a binary concept. Also, it can be temporary or permanent. Further, as Roth and his colleagues argue, it can be shown to be an empirically reliable concept as it is used by psychiatrists.[10] Hence, if you 'hold information constant', understanding on the part of the patient can be measured and used as an empirical measure of competence. Dr Harper's paper to this Conference refers to wishing to avoid a 'check list' for what is incompetence and what is competence; but perhaps we should, at least, look towards reliability of decision making about competence amongst ourselves as a profession, even if we do not believe it is a validatable concept.

CONCLUSION

Law and ethics are necessarily interrelated because of the breadth of legal definitions with which we are supplied and because there are substantive legal gaps. I would suggest that law and ethics are incongruous generally, almost inherently, one with the other. Hence, for example, in using the two ethical principles of autonomy and paternalism the law accepts that these two principles are the appropriate ones, but it rejects the notion that competence is a graded concept and it also rejects, essentially, the notion that autonomy and paternalism should be balanced against one another. The law regards things in as hierarchical way; it asks first, 'Is the patient competent?', if 'no', then 'this', if 'yes', then 'that'. Now I suggest that ordinary ethicists, such as ourselves, do not operate in this fashion. We use both concepts as graded concepts and, further, we balance one against the other in coming to what we consider to be correct ethical decisions. A colleague, Dr Tony Hope, and I published last year 'the balance model', which was a simple mathematical expression of what we believe most 'ethical deciders' do.[11] Clinical ethical committees (such as Professor Murphy has suggested to this Conference) are, of course, corporate examples of such 'ethical deciders'. We hope to carry out empirical work to confirm the anecdotal view that 'deciders' balance the level of autonomy that a patient can operate (how incompetent (s)he is) against how adverse are the consequences of not intervening. In the real ethical world I think that is how most of us operate.

In conclusion I do not think that there is a 'grey area' between ethics and the law. I believe there is actually inherent ethico-legal incongruence and I certainly believe that there is psycho-legal incongruence.

30

REFERENCES

1 Mental Health Act 1983.
2 *British Medical Journal* 1987;**296**:911–2.
3 World Medical Association, Declaration of Helsinki: 1964 (Revised 1975).
4 Meisel A, Roth L Z, Lidz C W. Toward a Model of the Legal Doctrine of Informed Consent. *American Journal of Psychiatry* 1977;**134**:285–9.
5 *Bolam v Friern Hospital Management Committee*, [1987] 2 All ER 118, [1957] I WLR 582.
6 *Sidaway v Bethlem Royal and Maudsley Hospitals* [1985] 2 WLR 480.
7 *Freeman v Home Office* [1983] 3 All ER 589.
8 Mental Health Act 1983, Sections 57 and 58.
9 Roth L H, Meisel A, Lidz C W. Tests of Competency to Consent to Treatment. *American Journal of Psychiatry* 1977;**134**:279–84.
10 Roth L H, Lidz C W, Meisel A, Soloff P H, Kaufman K, Spiker D G, Foster F G. Competency to Decide About Treatment or Research: an overview of some empirical data. *International Journal of Law and Psychiatry 1* 1982;**5**:29–50.
11 Eastman N L G, Hope R A. The Ethics of Enforced Medical Treatment: the balance model. *Journal of Applied Philosophy*. 1988; Vol 5, No 1.

DISCUSSION

Audience   What is the law's attitude to 'informed consent' and how explicitly are we bound to it?

Dr Eastman   The answer is straightforward, we do not have a doctrine of 'informed consent' in this country. In the two cases to which I referred, *Bolam and Sidaway*, the standard of consent, and specifically the standard of information requirement, amounts essentially to that of 'what is normal professional practice' for that situation. This contrasts with the alternative standard of 'that which the average patient needs to operate their autonomy'. That latter standard is the basis of the 'informal consent' doctrine and does apply in some states in the USA. It does not apply in England and Wales, except where it is determined by the court that the generally accepted professional standard in a particular medical situation operates at too low a level; then the courts reserve to themselves the right to decide that ordinary basic human autonomy cannot function and that consent is therefore not attained.

Audience   Concerning HIV testing; how do you deal with the patient who withdraws consent after the result is known, claiming he did not give consent in the first place?

I have been told by the Mental Welfare Commission in Scotland that, in general, cases requiring consent, e.g. ECT, consent is also required from the relatives, signed in the presence of the patient. A form has been devised in which the patient consents and then the relatives consent side by side, and this is witnessed by one of the medical staff. Is this legal or not?

Dr Eastman   As regards the withdrawing of consent as you describe it, I made the distinction earlier between the fact of consent and evidence as to the fact of consent. Where consent is withdrawn after a procedure has been carried out then the court decision will be based entirely on the presence or absence of evidence that consent was given at the time of the procedure.

Your second point questioned whether an ordinary consent form for ECT, or whatever, should be clarified by not only having the patient's signature but also a relative's. I do not think that is normal practice south of the border. Such a procedure can merely add weight to the evidential value of the consent form, by suggesting that it is clear that the patient consented.

CONSENT IN MENTAL HANDICAP

Professor Joan Bicknell
Professor of Psychiatry of Mental Handicap
St George's Hospital Medical School, London

INTRODUCTION

Consent is concerned with choosing between two or more options. For people with learning difficulties, such choices largely involve issues of life style and social matters, not medical questions. Children with learning difficulties have the same procedures available to them as children of normal intelligence. The parents make consent decisions by proxy or 'surrogate consent', but if the parents are not available or are incompetent, the procedures of wardship or reception into care are available. For parents of a child with a profound and multiple handicap the dilemmas are much more difficult, although the procedures are the same for the giving of consent. There will be uncharted medical territory for the family who face questions about life saving operations for the child who is severely handicapped. Operations with an uncertain outcome aimed to help with secondary handicaps will perplex some parents, and so will the pressure perceived by families of children with rare syndromes for their child to take part in research, which may be of no use to that child. There are very few children with handicaps abandoned in hospital now, but for those, reception into care procedures can be used. There is no need for the physician superintendent or consultant paediatrician to become paternalistic in making decisions about consent.

At 16 years the law dictates that the child becomes an adult. Some of those with learning difficulties will not be able to give consent, and will be described as legally incompetent. This happens not only to the person with mental handicap. Those with long term and disabling mental illnesses, some following head injury and those with dementia can also pose the same dilemmas.

There is a vacuum in the law for the adult who cannot give consent. Parents cannot give consent but it is good practice to have their agreement. The 1959 Mental Health Act provided the system of guardianship and thereby consent forms could be signed by the guardian for adults who were legally incompetent. It would be wrong to suggest that guardianship solved many problems: hardly any guardianship orders were served under the 1959 Mental Health Act and the 1983 Mental Health Act took away the right of the guardian to give consent. The power of the Court under 'Parens Patriae' and the royal prerogative is often quoted but the last warrant issued under that legal system was in 1960 and the procedure is no longer available. Advocates cannot help with consent at the moment and nor can the care giver. The Court of Protection cannot help. One system that has been used is for the various parties to go to the Law for a declaration based on the double negative that a certain procedure would not be unlawful. This is a way round the accusation that the intervention could be interpreted as a form of battery without consent.

THE CONSENT PROCESS

Is there anything that can be done to improve the legal competence of a mentally handicapped person? The form of the dialogue that takes place in the process of decision making, the complexity of the choices and the nature of the intellectual handicap clearly require further dissection. People with learning difficulties will need encouragement to be more autonomous if they are to be more competent in the making of choices. Such people have a wide range of learning difficulties; those who are profoundly handicapped may function intellectually as tiny babies even in adulthood, while those with mild intellectual handicap are at work and perhaps marrying and having families of their own. This group must not be thought of as homogeneous, having one life style or one set of competencies. This view leads to erroneous thinking such as the surgeon who may believe that a mentally handicapped patient cannot give consent by definition, the label automatically enforcing incompetence which may be erroneous. However, some generalisations are useful guidelines. Many people with mild mental handicap can give consent. Many people with moderate mental handicap can give consent if the choice is simple and many people with severe and profound mental handicap cannot give consent and will not be able to however much they are helped.

Consideration must be given to the opportunities that the individual has had for learning to make choices in his life and what results he has experienced. In one paternalistic long stay hospital, it was considered imperative, once a client had spent all his pocket money, that he was given extra money the following day to go to bingo. It was felt unfair, because he was mentally handicapped, for him to miss bingo and to feel the consequences of having spent his money all on one day. Most would think now that a useful learning opportunity had been missed in the management of his money.

The nature of the choice is also important. How many variables should be introduced? Are they concrete or abstract concepts? How much is the choice part of daily life? A children's home with many multiply handicapped children has introduced choices into the breakfast table routine. 'Is it to be Marmite or jam?' There are two jars and the child can point if he cannot speak, or use his eyes. There is also the possibility of butter only if no choice is made when it could be! Conversely, to ask people who have lived in hospital all their life whether they would like to leave and live in a group home which they have never seen will be fruitless and if a choice is made, cannot be considered valid.

What are the risks involved in allowing the client to make a choice? Is the wrong choice going to be catastrophic? The concept of sterilisation as a means of preventing pregnancy and allowing the individual permanent, trouble free, unprotected sexual intercourse will not be understood by many, even with mild intellectual handicap. It is too complex, abstract and the consequences are both short and long term and hard to visualise. The penalties of a possible pregnancy and what should be done about that or hypertension with long term oral contraception may simply add to the confusion in the decision making process. Yet even such a complex decision could be presented in a way that some will understand if the dialogue is with someone who knows the client and who is trusted by her. Some decisions are obviously wrong and will need to be overruled. The refusing of antibiotics in septicaemia could lead to a cerebral abscess and the refusal of an appendicectomy in acute appendicitis, on the basis that the operation may hurt, may lead to death. The risks involved in wrong decision making in these examples are very different from experiencing the wrong decision of having chosen a boring film as opposed to one which is exciting, but the concept of the mistaken decision is far better learned in the cinema than in the operating theatre. Finally, how complex is the topic? Five holiday brochures ranging from 'Outward Bound' in the Lake District to trips requiring a flight to Spain and living in a hotel may totally swamp the client and, unhelped, he may be made the more incompetent by the amount and complexity of the information produced.

When a decision has to be made or consent obtained from a mentally handicapped person the explanation should be given by someone known and trusted. The client's attention must be gained and short, simple, clear sentences used without leading questions. If presenting two options in a sentence and echolalia is suspected, the question should be turned round to see if the answer changes. Echolalia will invalidate most answers to direct questions. It is often useful to have a second person present in dialogues leading to decisions to study the non-verbal communication. The observation of this person can make the correct outcome clearer. The client may be over compliant. It is mutually very seductive for the handicapped person to be a passive victim of the lifestyle that has been chosen for him and for his care giver to be paternalistic. This sets the scene for the unscrupulous to use persuasive techniques.

There is very little research on the nature of such a dialogue that takes place with a person with learning difficulties who is being encouraged to make a choice but it is clear that the quality of such an interaction will render him either more or less competent to do so.

IMPLICIT CONSENT

The concept of implied consent is important in services which work with very severely handicapped people. Consent implied by lack of objection is used all the time. Meals are eaten, tablets are swallowed, clothes are changed and visits made to the toilet, or may be initiated by staff with usually no difficulty because the client does not object and has learned to do as he is told. This implicit consent must not be abused and there should be concern that contraceptives for example, may be handed out either with no explanation or with clients being told they are vitamin pills.

The doctrines of necessity and negligence and 'acting in good faith' and 'showing a duty of care' are important ethical guidelines when working with people who cannot make decisions for themselves and yet may have very little sense of self preservation. A client who runs away and has no road sense may decide to stroll down the central reservation of a motorway. The care giver is faced with two possibilities. He will either return willingly or struggle and kick when he is brought back against his will. The central reservation of a motorway is not the right place for him to be and the expected response from care givers is clear that he must return to safer ground, with or without his compliance.

Occasionally decisions have to be overridden. It may be obvious that the client has made the wrong decision because the likely outcome of various alternatives cannot be seen. For example, not wanting an appendicectomy because it will hurt, but not knowing that the alternative is death due to peritonitis. Both a client and his family may refuse to leave a long stay hospital; a hospital existence is wanted for the son or daughter, and yet the hospital is closing.

PROSPECTIVE CONSENT

There are forms that relatives or parents are made to sign when their son or daughter goes into respite or long term care in some establishments. The signature means for example that he can go riding, he can go on picnics, he can go on the river, he can have his teeth and his appendix out. Life style issues and medical questions are on the same form. The fact that the parent's consent is invalid is not apparently understood. The parents are told that without a signature the place is not available. These are real threats to placement and occur even today. Prospective consent is an important issue as it is invalid and ethically unacceptable. It allows the new care givers to be both judge and jury.

SPURIOUS CONSENT

The 'double negative' letter is often used in medical circles. 'Dear Doctor, Your client needs an appointment in the ENT Department and unless I hear from you to the contrary I will make that appointment.' This is an abuse of the concept of consent. It relies on the other party's inertia in letter writing and is a sad reflection on the standard of correspondence in medical care today. It is used not only with medical issues: 'Dear Mrs Smith, ... Hospital is closing and we wish to make a video as an historic record. Unless we hear from you to the contrary, your son, John, will be videoed.' The expected lack of response may be due to illiteracy, a change of address or lack of interest but implied agreement is hardly justified in this manoeuvre. Major and justified criticism was meted out to those who conducted one of the first large measles vaccine trials, based on consent implied from the non response of parents of mentally handicapped children.

PATERNALISM AND AUTONOMY

These are central issues when working with people with learning difficulties, linked very much to the philosophy of normalisation which for some has become an ideology, never to be questioned. For most people with learning difficulties, there needs to be a fine balance between a father-like approach from the care giver as to a child and encouragement to the client to acquire the thoughts and skills of an adult and to become as autonomous as possible. This fine balance will change in time and according to circumstances and may even need to change in the space of one day. The philosophy of normalisation values autonomy rather than paternalism which has brought a great deal of good to human services but an extreme view can be damaging. A family was distressed because their daughter was to live in a hostel where there had been a series of road traffic accidents because it was assumed that these clients with learning difficulties were safe on the road as autonomous adults. It had been overlooked that there had been no road safety programmes for the clients in previous placements and they were not autonomous as expected to be. When ideology overshadows reality the balance between necessary paternalism and autonomy can be misjudged, abusing the clients and the trust they place in their care givers.

BEHAVIOURAL MODIFICATION PROGRAMMES

Many of these are complex, and are pervasive of every aspect of life, particularly those using token economy. Many therapists have had the experience of setting up contracts with mildly handicapped people who have agreed to go on such programmes, where it was felt that they had sufficient understanding of the issues. But there is tremendous pressure from some organisations that handicapped people, by definition, should not be signing contracts. Many more behavioural programmes are carried out on those who cannot give consent and the ethical issues here are great and should be the concern of more people than the therapists themselves. It must be remembered that while many of these behaviour programmes are at present done in hospital, they will be set up more and more in the community where the acquisition of support and supervision is going to be a very different exercise.

DISHONESTY AND CHOICE

Dishonesty sometimes slips into the area of contracts, decision making, choice and consent, sadly fuelled sometimes by the simplicity of our clients and the gullibility of care givers. Consider the dilemma of the client who frequently runs away but if he wears his slippers he does not do so. This is because as a little boy he was taught not to wear his slippers outside. He is made to wear slippers during the day time which means that the doors can stand open with the sunshine and fresh air pouring in. It is the least restrictive alternative, but it is dishonest which should be acknowledged. A far more serious example is the performing of a hysterectomy when sterilisation is the goal. Sterilisation is seen to be controversial and to have eugenic overtones from which staff may shy away, sometimes to the detriment of the client. No one likes being associated with problems that smack of racial hygiene nor do care givers choose to be associated with a decision that is seen by others to be devaluing the client group. It is much easier to accept the decision for a hysterectomy, possibly on the grounds of exaggerated symptoms, despite that operation being much bigger and causing much more discomfort.

CONCLUSION

People with learning difficulties need to learn to make choices from an early age; remember the Marmite and the jam. They need help to experience the consequences of small decisions; if two day's pocket money is spent today, then let there be no more money tomorrow. Parents need help to understand the legal situation: many do not and are quite rightly distressed if the legal aspects are explained in a bland, unsympathetic and uncaring manner. They feel that they are being pushed out of the decision making process and yet they suspect that they will be left with a large part of the caring or perhaps all of it if things go wrong. The care givers' role as proxy decision makers must be taken seriously and procedures must be clarified. Make sure that the local District General Hospital knows what to do about consent forms for adults with learning difficulties who are legally incompetent. The procedures must be given dignity and paediatric consent forms should not be used.

Know when to resort to formal legal involvement. Questions of sterilisation of women with learning difficulties must always be taken to the law but in most other circumstances there are ways of managing a situation which avoids an expensive, time consuming, stressful legal process which may invade the privacy of the client and possibly the family.

Above all let us value the clients that we serve. Let us encourage them in decision making, but if it is not possible, let us make decisions on their behalf with honesty, respect and humility. Let us be aware of the tremendous responsibility that we carry on their behalf.

FURTHER READING

Consent & The Incompetent. *Institute of Medical Ethics Bulletin* 1988; No. 47: 3.
Report of the Working Party on the Legal, Medical & Ethical Issues of Mental Handicap. Competency And Consent To Medical Treatment. MENCAP, 1989.
Gillon R. On Sterilising Severely Mentally Handicapped People. *Journal of Medical Ethics Editorial* 1987;**13**:59–61.
Section for the Psychiatry of Mental Handicap. Interim Guidelines on Consent to Medical and Surgical Treatment, Contraception, Sterilisation and Abortion in the Mentally Handicapped. *Bulletin of the Royal College of Psychiatrists* 1986; **10**:184.
Memorandum by The Law Society's Mental Health Sub Committee. Decision-making and Mental Incapacity: A Discussion Document. January 1989.

PSYCHIATRIC DISORDER IN PRISON

Dr M Swinton and Dr T Maden
Department of Forensic Psychiatry
Institute of Psychiatry, London

The Department of Forensic Psychiatry at the Institute of Psychiatry is currently working on a study of psychiatric disorder amongst sentenced prisoners. This paper attempts to cover some of the issues concerning the location of severely mentally ill people in prison. My remarks will be limited to people who are in prison because they have received prison sentences and not to those held on remand.

There has been considerable concern about prison overcrowding and the steadily rising prison population. There is a widely held belief that there are large numbers of people who are inappropriately in prison when they should instead be under psychiatric care. It has been argued that there is a direct causal link between the reduced numbers in psychiatric hospital and the rising prison population.[1]

What is not actually known is the current nature and extent of psychiatric disorder in the sentenced prisoner population. For example, for people with major and chronic illnesses such as schizophrenia it is not known how many cases there are in prison and whether they are recognised cases who have gone to prison because no hospital would take them or perhaps they have slipped undetected into prison or even become ill in prison.

There have been a number of previous studies in this area and Figure 1 shows most of the major UK studies.[2-8] They have used differing samples and methodology but produce broadly comparable results: rates of psychotic mental illness in the 1–2% range, rates of neurotic illness no higher than the 10–12% similar to that found in community studies, high rates of personality disorder, alcohol and drug dependency and raised rates of mental handicap.

Most of these studies (apart from the last) were done in single prisons on people recently entering prison. Prisons are in fact very varied in the type of person they hold and these studies tend to contain mainly short term prisoners who are not necessarily representative of the population as a whole.

Our own study aims to remedy these difficulties and it involves our interviewing a representative sample of 5% of sentenced prisoners of all types and at all stages of sentence. We will use this sample to estimate the nature and extent of psychiatric disorder in the total population. We will assess need for treatment for all cases and identify areas of unmet need for psychiatric treatment within that population. When our results become available they will give a cross-sectional view of the population but they will not show how the population is changing with time. There is however some information available on the changes in the numbers of the mentally disordered population in prison over the past 10 years.

STUDIES OF PSYCHIATRIC DISORDER IN UK PRISONS			
Roper	1950	Wakefield	1100 males
Gibbens	1953	Feltham	200 male youths
Robinson	1965	Belfast	566 males
Bluglass	1966	Perth	300 males
Faulk	1976	Winchester	72 males
Washbrook	1977	Birmingham	1800 males
Gunn	1980	South East	106 males

Figure 1.

DETAINABLE MENTALLY DISORDERED INMATES
SENTENCED ONLY

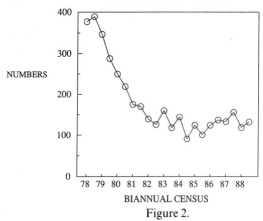

Figure 2.

Every six months since 1979 the Prison Medical Service has conducted a census of the numbers of sentenced inmates who are thought to be detainable under the Mental Health Act. (This includes mental illness, psychopathic disorder and mental impairment). (Figure 2. Source: Home Office figures) The medical officer for each prison is the source of the data. The census data needs cautious interpretation given that the information comes from so many sources and it is possible that not all patients with severe and chronic mental illnesses such as schizophrenia are considered detainable by the prison medical officers. Nevertheless this data gives some indication of changes occurring over time in the numbers of the most unwell of all mentally disordered prisoners.

The first point to be made from this data is that throughout the past decade there have been at any one time between 100 and 200 mentally disordered individuals who are in prison serving sentences when they should clearly be in hospital. The second and more surprising point is that since 1981 this population has been fairly stable. The figures give no support to the argument that the number of mentally ill prisoners is rising rapidly. It is however possible that at the same time there has been a rise in the numbers of mentally ill prisoners who have not been considered to be detainable by the prison doctors—and thus not appeared in the figures.

In the period between the start of the census in 1978 and 1981 there was a sharp fall in the population. The reasons for this fall are not clear. If it is assumed that the total number of mentally disordered committing crimes and coming to trial remained fairly static over this time then the population of detainable mentally disordered prisoners becoming sentenced prisoners could only fall if more were receiving hospital orders from court or more were being transferred to hospital on remand or after sentence (i.e. Section 37, 48 and 47 of the 1983 Act and Section 60, 73 and 72 of the 1957 Act). During this period there was indeed a small rise in the number of Section 73 and 72 transfers (from 61 to 107) but at the same time there was a decrease in the number of Section 60 hospital orders (from 657 to 637). Therefore transfer of patients to hospital does not appear to account for this fall which must be due to other factors.

Such statistics would be meaningless if the prison doctors were missing large numbers of cases. It seems to be a common belief that there are many mentally ill persons who get lost and ignored in prison. The idea is that such people are locked in a cell and their disturbed mental state never comes to the attention of doctors. In clinical practice outside prison people are sometimes seen who have been psychotic for a long time without coming to the attention of medical services. They are people who are living alone, perhaps not looking after themselves, but spending most of their time indoors and not doing anything to bring attention to themselves. However, it is very difficult for this to happen inside prison. People who have not visited prisons do not always realise how intimately life is lived inside. Prisoners are rarely alone. Most have to share their cell with at least one other person. When they are out of their cell they have to conform to a highly structured routine and obey a large number of rules. People who cannot conform or who behave in an unusual manner very quickly come to the attention of other inmates and staff. Such people will be subject to ridicule from other inmates. Staff quickly recognise the prisoner who does not fit although they may not always recognise the mental disorder causing this. The prison doctor soon becomes involved in such a case. Prison staff may refer such a person to the doctor if they think him ill. Alternatively if such a person has committed an offence against prison rules a punishment can then be imposed by the governor. In these cases the prison doctor must see such a person first to rule out clinical contraindications to punishment. Therefore cases of mental illness will usually come rapidly to the attention of the prison doctor. Of course doctors can still miss the diagnosis and attribute the problem behaviour to other factors but overall it seems unlikely that many cases of severe mental illness will go unnoticed in prison.

I have used these figures in order to play down the exaggerated ideas that are current about vast numbers of patients being in prison but I do not wish to give the impression that there are no problems with the numbers of mentally ill currently in prison. If 1–2% of sentenced prisoners do have chronic psychotic mental disorders (including here both those who could be considered 'detainable' and those who could not) that would be 370–740 people locked up today in the prisons of England and Wales. While this is a small number in terms of all the psychiatric patients in the country this is clearly a group with very special needs and it is of course a large number in relationship to the number of Forensic Psychiatry beds in the country.

The question that can be asked for this group is whether it is wrong that they are in prison. Firstly it can be argued that these people are responsible for their actions and secondly that the treatment they can get in prison is as good as that outside. In our research so far we have come across medical court reports where it is argued that someone may have schizophrenia but that at the time of the offence they had no psychotic symptoms therefore the offence had nothing to do with their illness and they were responsible for their actions. A similar line of argument is that the person has schizophrenia but also has a personality disorder and this is the cause of their offending. Arguments about legal responsibility are always complex but it is surprising to see reports which totally ignore the disabling symptoms of chronic schizophrenia. It would be foolish to argue that someone with schizophrenia should never be sent to prison for an offence but this should surely be something that happens only rarely.

Moving on to the second argument—that people with schizophrenia can be treated just as well in prison; this comes down to the idea that the only treatment for schizophrenia is neuroleptics which can be prescribed anywhere. Yet, of course, hospital treatment involves much more than neuroleptics and the fact is that resources such as occupational therapy and social work are not widely available to sentenced prisoners. In addition, mentally ill prisoners are subject at times to considerable harassment from other inmates. Thus people with schizophrenia who are in prison are unable to get the treatment they could get outside prison. Certainly in our study we are working on the basis that people with chronic mental illnesses in general should not be in prison.

CONCLUSION

There appears little evidence that there are large and growing numbers of people with serious mental illnesses who have been given prison sentences. Nevertheless there does appear to be a small group in this position. Our research will clarify the clinical needs of this population and describe how these needs can best be met.

REFERENCES

1 Weller M P I, Weller B G A. Crime and mental illness. *Medicine Science and the Law* 1988;**1**:38–45.
2 Roper W F. A comparative study of the Wakefield Prison population in 1948. (Part 1) *British Journal of Delinquency* 1950;**1**:15–28. (Part 2) *British Journal of Delinquency* 1950;**1**:243–70.
3 Gibbens T C N. Psychiatric studies of Borstal lads. OUP: Maudsley Monograph No 11, 1963.
4 Robinson C B, Patten J W, Kerr W S. A psychiatric assessment of criminal offenders. *Medicine Science and the Law* 1965;**5**:140–6.
5 Bluglass R. A psychiatric study of Scottish convicted prisoners. MD thesis, University of St Andrews, 1966.
6 Faulk M. A psychiatric study of men serving a sentence in Winchester Prison. *Medicine Science and Law* 1976;**16**:244–61.
7 Washbrook R A H. The psychiatrically ill prisoner. *Lancet* 1977;**i**:1302–3.
8 Gunn J, Robertson G, Dell S, Way G. Psychiatric aspects of imprisonment. London: Academic Press, 1980.

DRUG MISUSE AND THE LAW

Dr John Strang

Consultant Psychiatrist

Drug Dependence Research and Treatment Unit

Maudsley Hospital, London

In the next 3 papers some specific areas of overlap between drug use and the law will be considered. It is known that a proportion of prisoners have previously been involved in use of illicit drugs such as opiates. We must also consider the potential contact between drug users and the Criminal Justice system at earlier points in their drug careers. In the second paper, Dr Andrew Johns, Senior Lecturer in the Department of Addictive Behaviour at St George's Hospital in London reports on the results of a survey of the views of magistrates on the drug users who come before them. In the third paper, Dr Michael Gossop of the Drug Dependence Clinical Research and Treatment Unit at the Maudsley looks at the potential for creative therapeutic exploitation of the Criminal Justice System at a yet earlier point, as embodied in the Southwark Arrest Referral Scheme, in which we are looking to see the extent to which it is possible to divert drug users from their present path—to turn the event of arrest or cautioning into a 'healthy jolt' or 'therapeutic event'.

However, first of all I would like to consider whether the issue of drug users within the Criminal Justice System really warrants such attention—and, if so, why? HIV and AIDs are forcing a fundamental re-examination of goals and strategies in responding to drug users at various levels. One particular area of concern is that drug use may be continuing within the prison system. At the Thomas Okey Memorial Lecture at the Institute of Psychiatry it was Dr Stimson's opinion that we were at a point of crisis, a point of change between paradigms.[1] Hence it is so important to examine the various points of contact with drug users.

The Criminal Justice System, and in particular the prison system, is an enormously important point of contact with drug users. At a time when there are urgent requirements being identified by reports such as the two reports on AIDS and Drug Misuse from the Advisory Council on Misuse of Drugs, we must look again at the main points of contact within the overall system.[2,3] How many drug users are there in prison? There is little data available and reports such as Dr Swinton's will be necessary to inform discussions and decisions over the next year or so. Each year about 3000 offenders receive custodial sentences for drug offences, almost all of whom will have received these sentences for charges relating to heroin or cocaine. A survey conducted in the prison system in mid-1987 found that at one point in time there were three and a half thousand prisoners who were in prison for a drugs offence.[4] It is evident that there are additionally a large number of drug users who have been

44

imprisoned for offences which are not recorded as a drug offence—various forms of 'acquisitive crimes': even breaking into a pharmacy is not recorded as a drugs offence. There will additionally be those held on remand. Thus it might be reasonable to presume that of the 50 000 prison population at any one time at least 10% may be former drug users. Might there be other ways in which a drug user could be identified in the prison system—what about medical examination? The 1986 report from the Social Services Committee on the Prison Medical Service identified an average length of time of 72 seconds for a medical examination which they regarded as 'often perfunctory or useless'.[5] Notifications to the Home Office Addicts Index contained only slightly more than 1000 notifications last year (1988)—surely a gross underestimate given the earlier figures.[6] However, it may well be that there is a different reason for low identification—the lack of any incentive to self-disclosure. It is widely believed by drug users that no significant or relevant treatment would be provided for their withdrawal distress; might it be the case that self-disclosure and hence recognition of drug users might be greater if there was a greater willingness on the part of police surgeons and prison medical officers to provide treatments such as an opiate withdrawal schedule (as recommended by the Department of Health's Medical Working Group on Drug Dependence; 1984).[7]

The failure to intervene at this level constitutes a major deficiency in strategies to combat the spread of HIV/AIDS. It may well be that lack of appropriate treatment fuels the fire of HIV by encouraging use of black market drugs such as heroin in prisons. It must be remembered that one is trying to control a drug that is certainly easy to conceal and pass over. Of particular concern is the possibility that prisoners may engage in atypical behaviour when in prison—such as homosexual activity including unprotected anal intercourse in previously exclusively heterosexual males. However, more directly relevant to our considerations is that the sharing of needle and syringe by drug users who had previously not injected or had injected but not shared may occur when they are in the unusual circumstances of prison.

What are the factors bearing on HIV risk in the prison system with regard to drug use? Of course, it is not the drugs themselves that constitute the HIV threat (Figure 1). Figure 1 is a graphical representation, with the extent of HIV risk from drug use on the vertical axis, and the horizontal axis being the extent of black market availability of various products within a prison—perhaps starting with more easily concealed items such as the drugs themselves (in the area marked A) moving on to more difficult items such as needles and syringes (marked B). The analysis for a particular prison is difficult: at a time when no injecting equipment at all is available (A on the horizontal axis), then drug-related HIV risk would appear to be minimal. However, as soon as one needle and syringe enter the system, then HIV risk becomes near maximal, and this is compatible with anecdotal reports from drug users of sharing in unhygienic circumstances when in prison, using borrowed equipment which has become blunt with use by dozens of previous inmates. Then as needle and syringe availability becomes even greater, the HIV risk from each event of sharing might become less as well-used, and hence high-risk, equipment is replaced by

45

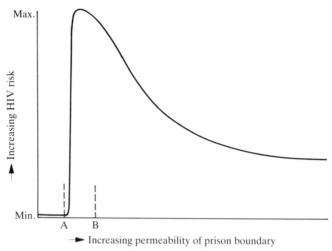

Figure 1. Graphical representation of changing HIV risk for imprisoned drug addict with changing levels of permeability of prison boundaries/control.

new. Thus the shape and in particular the height of the peak of this curve might be capable of modification by the provision of information about the means of cleaning needles and syringes, accompanied by real access to opportunities to implement such cleaning without detection.

Finally, I would like to consider two important characteristics of the drug-taking behaviour—its *variability* and *malleability*. Drug use is not synonymous with drug dependence. Within the population in prisons there will be those whose drug use falls into a variety of different categories. There will be those who have been experimental users in the past and possibly within the prison system, who are using out of curiosity there will be those who then make a balanced decision to continue with use, perhaps on an occasional basis, whom one might regard as recreational users; there will then be compulsive dependent users who have got into difficulties with their drug use, who are the group that Dr Swinton and Dr Maden were referring to earlier. Even within compulsive use, we find considerable variability. In an unpublished survey by Alistair Stewart and myself of 56 herion addicts presenting to services in Manchester in 1985, we found that 18 (about a third) had not injected at all in the last month, but that of those who were injecting virtually all had shared at one time or another. Such sharing was by no means universal, with only half of these 'sharers' having shared in the last month. Similarly in the data from our community drug team at the Maudsley, we find that about half of the heroin addicts are primarily injectors, and the other half are primarily taking their heroin only by 'chasing the dragon'.[8]

There is considerable evidence of movement between different patterns of use, and this is perhaps the key point—that it appears that there may be

46

considerable malleability in a drug habit. In a two-year follow-up study in Manchester a large cohort of drug users was traced, 55 of whom were still using drugs. However, the nature of their drug use had changed considerably.[9] They were initially assigned to 3 different dose categories, and half of them reduced their dose—in other words they had gone back up the slippery slope.

Frequency of injecting was examined, and 23 of them (nearly half of them) had reduced their frequency of injecting—including 11 who had stopped completely—even though they continued to use the drugs by other routes.

Thus in conclusion, it would appear to be well within the repertoire of many drug users to mould or modify the nature of their ongoing drug use according to the circumstances. The challenge for society must be to find ways in which the circumstances may be used to promote identifiable behaviour change to reduce not only the overall extent of drug use, but also the HIV-risk laden nature of the behaviour.

REFERENCES

1 Stimson G V. HIV and AIDS. *British Journal of Addiction* (in press).
2 Advisory Council on the Misuse of Drugs. AIDS and Drug Misuse: Part I. London: HMSO, 1988.
3 Advisory Council on the Misuse of Drugs. AIDS and Drug Misuse: Part 2. London: HMSO, 1989.
4 Tippell S. Drug Users and the Prison System. In: Drugs and British Society: Responses to a Social Problem in the 1980s (ed MacGregor S). London: Rontledge, 1989.
5 House of Commons Social Services Committee. The Prison Medical Service: Third Report from the Social Services Committee. London: HMSO, 1986.
6 Home Office. Statistics on the Misuse of Drugs in the UK. London: HMSO, 1989.
7 Department of Health and Social Services. Guidelines of Good Clinical Practice in the Management of Drug Misuse. London: DHSS, 1984.
8 Gossop M, Griffiths P, Strang J. 'Chasing the dragon': characteristics of heroin chasers. *British Journal of Addiction* 1988;**83**:1115–62.
9 Strang J, Heathcote S, Watson P. Habit moderation in injecting drug users. *Health Trends* 1987;**19**:16–8.

DRUG USE, CRIME AND THE VIEWS OF MAGISTRATES

Dr Andrew Johns
Senior Lecturer
Department of Addictive Behaviour
St George's Hospital Medical School, London

BACKGROUND TO THE STUDY

Those who work with drug users rapidly become aware that many of them are in regular contact with the criminal justice system. Each assessment of a new client involves a detailed exploration of the previous record of offending, recent offences and any cases which may be outstanding. The extent of this involvement is also brought home by frequent requests by magistrates and probation officers for preparation of psychiatric reports on the drug using offender. Workers in busy clinical settings may feel that they are in contact with large numbers of drug users and that this represents the commonest response to drug problems in this country. However, there are good reasons for believing that the national response to drug problems is not medical, but judicial. More drug users are likely to present to magistrates' courts than to drug treatment clinics. For example, in 1987, over 23 000 people were convicted or cautioned for drug offences, whilst in the same year, 10 700 addicts were notified to the Home Office. There are, however, good reasons for supposing that both of these figures are underestimates. Much of the crime related to drug use does not feature in official statistics. For example, much acquisitive crime, such as theft, burglary and shoplifting, may be committed to sustain drug use but is not recorded as such. Parker and Newcombe conducted a survey of crime in the Wirral and found that in a consecutive series of 100 people convicted of burglary, half of them were independently known to drug treatment agencies as opioid users.[1]

Furthermore, notification rates are known to be low. Although it is the legal duty of any doctor to notify the Home Office of addicts taking opiates and cocaine, fewer than one in five drug users may, in fact, be notified. Despite the limitations of these figures, it remains likely that the criminal justice system deals with more drug users than the health service.

For these reasons, the judicial response to drug use and drug related crime is of enormous national importance. However measured, crime related to drug use appears to be increasing. Over the last decade, the number of offences recorded as being related to drug use has increased by 200%, whereas indictable offences have shown a slight decrease over the same decade. Amongst offences related to drug use the commonest is possession. Of the total number of people convicted of drug related offences in 1987, 84% were convicted of possession, and 80% of these cases involved cannabis.

Given that drug users commit large amounts of crime and they present frequently to the courts, it becomes pertinent to follow their subsequent progress through the criminal justice system. As 90% of all crime and 80% of all drug related offences are dealt with by magistrates' courts, this then becomes the main arena in which criminal problems related to drug use are managed.

The attitudes of magistrates' to factors such as the relative seriousness of offences related to drug use, their perception of the responsibility of an offender for his/her actions, and the likely response to treatment, if any is contemplated, may all have a bearing on the disposal of the drug-using offender. In many of these cases a psychiatric report may be requested.

No previous survey has examined the views of magistrates on the problems related to crime and drug use. With the active help of the Magistrates' Association, the following study was designed to examine the views of a representative sample of the 3000 London magistrates on aspects of drug use and drug related crime.

A questionnaire was therefore devised which covered the following areas: the perceived seriousness of drug-use and offences related to drug-use; the personal responsibility of drug-users for their actions; the goals of treatment; the value of medical reports, sentencing options and probation orders.

RESULTS

The magistrates tended to agree that possession of heroin and cocaine was a serious matter. They also agreed that selling drugs between users was a serious offence, and they were in agreement that those who offended under the influence of heroin or cannabis were responsible for their actions.

There were however, some interesting areas of disagreement. For example, 70% thought that the possession of cannabis was a serious matter, whereas a third of the sample did not. On the matter of responsibility for statements made during withdrawal, the magistrates were divided. A third of them thought that heroin users were responsible, a third did not know, and a third said the addicts were not responsible for statements made at times of withdrawal.

The magistrates also had mixed views on the value of various disposal options. Regarding prison, suspended or deferred sentences and probation, nearly a third of the magistrates did not think they had much value. However, when asked the specific question: 'Do you think that probation is a good idea when it is combined with a condition of treatment?', an overwhelming majority, 92%, agreed.

Regarding treatment goals, while a quarter of magistrates thought that long-term provision of drugs may be necessary, most supported abstinence as a goal and identified specialists as best placed to undertake this treatment. They had some interesting views on the value of psychiatric reports; half of the sample thought that the reports were not clearly worded, contained too much medical jargon or were partial to the defendant.

49

DISCUSSION

Although a third of the magistrates did not think that possession of cannabis for personal use was a serious matter, this comprises 80% of all drugs offences. It may be asked if this is an appropriate response, when the misuse of other drugs is perceived as a greater national problem and a higher national priority. Many police forces regard possession of cannabis as less serious than possession of other substances and this is reflected in an increased use of a caution, usually for first time offenders found in possession of cannabis for personal use.

The magistrates' views on responsibility of offenders for their actions are worthy of comment. A third of the magistrates thought that a statement made during a period of withdrawal was not valid, whereas a third did not know, and a third thought that the drug user was still responsible. This is an area where some medical research can help to clarify matters because there is no doubt that withdrawal from some drugs of dependence can produce an altered mental state, which may subsequently affect the admissibility of the evidence. If someone who is in the early stages of dependence on alcohol, commits a driving offence and subsequently gives a statement, it is unlikely that mild symptoms of withdrawal from alcohol would so impair his mental state as to make that statement inadmissable in court. However, marked dependence on drugs such as opiates, benzodiazepines or barbiturates may, in some cases, produce a withdrawal state which does affect subsequent admissibility. There is a need for magistrates and police to be aware of this fact and to request a medical opinion or report when necessary.

Regarding disposal options, the divergence of views between magistrates is fascinating in that a third of all magistrates have reservations about custodial and noncustodial sentences, including probation. While the punitive aspect of these sentences is clearly important, the magistrates are presumably pessimistic about the ability of prison and probation to reform the drug-using offender. They seem to be saying 'we know that prison or probation is necessary in many cases, but we don't feel that the drug-user is going to be helped to change by these forms of disposal.'

Nearly all of the sample supported the sentence of 'probation with an attached condition of treatment', which is clearly a form of compulsory treatment. There is long experience in the United States of this form of intervention and a recent American review concluded that 'the criminal justice system is important in the identification and retention of drug abusers in treatment'.[2] In Britain compulsory treatment of addicts was proposed by a government advisory committee in 1965 but rejected. There are practically no treatment facilities for drug-users within British prisons though some agencies offer advice and support to drug using prisoners.

With the aim of reducing the prison population and drawing more drug-users into treatment, the Home Office has recently published a Green Paper *Punishment, Custody and the Community* (HMSO 1988). The government proposes to introduce a new order giving courts the power to place a range of

50

requirements on offenders who would otherwise be sent to jail, with specific proposals for the treatment of offending drug-users in the community.

Whatever the wishes of magistrates and notwithstanding the government proposals, most drug agencies believe that voluntary referral is a necessary part of the process of recovery and few are willing to take on clients as a condition of a court order. This is a problem that both medicine and the legal system need to address. While there may be a need for innovative use of probation orders, this can only come about and be properly evaluated if there is sensible co-operation between the courts and the medical system.

CONCLUSIONS

In summary, there are interesting differences of views between magistrates. Some of these divergences of view reflect the national debate on issues such as the seriousness of cannabis. In other cases, the differences of views between magistrates may reflect a lack of understanding of phenomena such as withdrawal states from drugs. Clearly there is a need for a better understanding between the courts and the treatment agencies of each others' role; and also for proper evaluation of the effects of closer collaboration on treatment and outcome.

ACKNOWLEDGEMENTS

This paper draws on research carried out in collaboration with Dr Michael Gossop, Research Psychologist Drug Dependence, Clinical Research and Treatment Unit, Bethlem Royal Hospital, Kent. The authors wish to thank the Magistrates' Association for their help.

FURTHER READING

Johns A R, Gossop M. Drug Use, Crime and The Attitudes of Magistrates. *Medicine, Science and The Law* (in press).

REFERENCES

1 Parker H, Newcombe R. Heroin Use and Acquisitive Crime in an English Community. *The British Journal of Sociology* 1987;**38**:331–50.
2 Johnson B. A view from America. Crime and Compulsory Treatment. *DRUGLINK* 1989;**4**:12–3.

DISCUSSION

Audience   Could you elaborate on your comments concerning compulsory treatment orders in drug users? How do you define drug user? Do you mean drug-related offences, or offences committed because of drug use? How do you identify a suitable case for treatment?

Dr Johns   Offences related to drug use fall into three categories. There are those offences committed whilst under the influence of the drug, offences committed to acquire a drug and 'technical' offences related to the physical possession, dealing and trafficking in drugs. The reality is that the courts and the judicial system are reasonably good at recognising drug users. The assessment of the problems of those drug users is relatively easily done: the probation office or the magistrates' court will often get in touch with the local psychiatric department. As to who may be an ideal candidate for conditional treatment, the answer is unknown because no such study has been undertaken in this country. My guess would be that in a carefully designed study, the drug using offender who had no offence prior to drug use may be the person who would be best helped by conditional treatment. It is known that four fifths of drug users have committed offences before they first use illicit drugs, and it would be naive to suppose that a conditional probation order, whatever its effect, would help such a person.

Audience   I would like to raise a point as a magistrate, not as a doctor; in your research, did you take into consideration whether these attitudes were expressed in relation to first offenders, or to persistent offenders? One of the big problems we find as magistrates is that you may adopt an entirely different attitude to a first offender, but when people come repeatedly into court, and various options have been tried, the law requires that you do something.

Dr Johns   I think that is a very valuable comment. We did not try and distinguish between first and repeated offenders because this was a preliminary survey of magistrates' views.

THE SOUTHWARK ARREST REFERRAL PROJECT

Dr Michael Gossop
Head of Research
Drug Dependence Clinical Research and Treatment Unit
Maudsley Hospital, London

Things have changed a great deal over the past few decades in this country. At the time of the original Brain Report and the creation of the drug clinics in this country at the end of the 1960s, there was no black market in heroin.[1] The clinic system was set up partly in order to prevent the development of such a black market. The current situation is very different, with a flourishing black market. There have been dramatic changes within the past decade particularly in the number of heroin addicts in this country. One of the important factors which influenced this development was the Iranian revolution. When the Ayatollah came to power he ejected the heroin manufacturers, who took their technology for producing heroin and moved into areas of Pakistan, Afghanistan and India. The heroin they produced from these areas, 'Pakistani' heroin, was of high quality compared to that previously available. One of its characteristics was that Pakistani heroin could be smoked. Traditionally the pattern of heroin addiction in this country was by injection. With the appearance of Pakistani heroin a new phenomenon was noticed, smoking heroin, 'chasing the dragon' as it is frequently called which is now well established.

Whether because the heroin was smokable or for other reasons, there was a rapid increase in the number of heroin abusers and a consequent increase in the number of addicts in this country. It has been suggested that taking heroin by intravenous injection represents a massive and significant first step which prevents people from moving into the use of heroin. The possibility of smoking heroin has made it less daunting to initial users and perhaps more people became experimenters and were trapped in the process.

The other significant development is the appearance of HIV infection. Intravenous drug abusers are at high risk with regard to HIV infection. There is evidence that the male homosexual community has changed its behaviour significantly with regard to high risk practices and is no longer a rapidly developing group with regard to infection. That is not true of injecting drug abusers. Since most injecting drug abusers are heterosexual these people may act as a bridgehead into the broader community.

These two factors together have been a powerful political motivating force which have contributed to a number of changes in our society's attitudes towards the problem. The changes in response that have been introduced are that there is general agreement that the types of treatment that are available for

53

WAYS OF FINANCING DRUG HABITS
(Self-Reported)

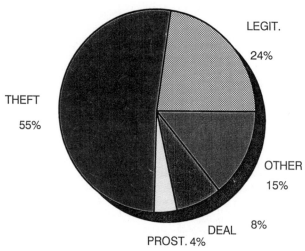

LEGIT.

24%

THEFT

55%

OTHER

15%

DEAL 8%
PROST. 4%

Figure 1. This figure shows the different ways in which drug addicts (predominantly heroin addicts) attending the Maudsley Community Drugs Team reported obtaining money to buy drugs. Theft stands out as the most common means (55%). Other methods include legitimate means (through money from jobs, private incomes, etc.), dealing in drugs, and prostitution. Note that the percentages given in the figure do not add up to 100 since more than one means could be reported by each subject.

drug problems should be broadened. We should move beyond the traditional, clinic based, medical model which was used throughout the 1970s and should be looking for different types of treatment interventions. There is a move towards preventive intervention. Alternatives to the existing types of treatment intervention need to be sought.

There is a large degree of overlap between the criminal justice system and the medical management of drug misuse. Many crimes are related to drug misuse of one sort or another. There are drug-related crimes of possession and of trafficking and selling. In studies of drug addicts high rates of convictions for drug-related crimes such as possession and dealing have been reported. One study found that 62% of their sample of addicts in treatment had been convicted of at least one directly drug-related offence,[2] and another also noted that 58% of a similar sample had at least one such conviction.[3] The most common crimes associated with drug taking are acquisition to pay for obtaining drugs. Drug addicts that I have seen indicate that theft and related crimes are the major method by which they obtain their drugs (Figure 1). Many of the people with drug problems were involved in criminal activities prior to their first use of drugs.

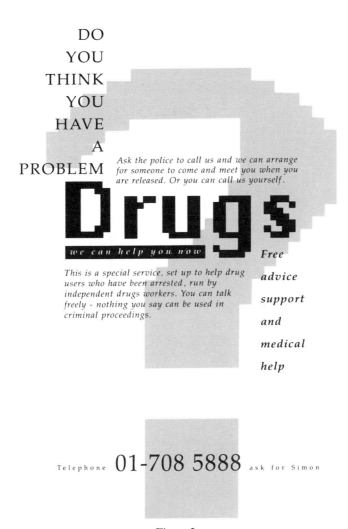

DO
YOU
THINK
YOU
HAVE
A
PROBLEM

Ask the police to call us and we can arrange
for someone to come and meet you when you
are released. Or you can call us yourself.

Drugs

we can help you now

Free

This is a special service, set up to help drug
users who have been arrested, run by
independent drugs workers. You can talk
freely - nothing you say can be used in
criminal proceedings.

advice

support

and

medical

help

Telephone 01-708 5888 ask for Simon

Figure 2.

The Southwark Arrest Referral Project is a short term pilot project funded over a period of one year based at Borough Police Station in Southwark. Southwark is a mixed area, a very poor area with a great deal of inner city deprivation. It has a lot of crime and drug taking and there are many heroin problems located in the borough. The scheme is funded by the Home Office and is based at one police station in Borough High Street. Every person who comes to Borough High Street who is charged with any offence will receive our card (Figure 2). There is no selection of people aimed at those who are charged with drug offences. The card is very simple, in effect it says, 'Do you have a drug problem? If so, this scheme exists where you can ring up a named person in confidence. Nothing that is said to him will be used in criminal proceedings.' There are large numbers of people passing through the police station and it should be possible to use this significant event to initiate contact with the treatment system. When people get in touch with 'Simon', who is the Arrest Referral Project worker, he provides them with information and advice. He is there to provide them with help insofar as he can, but more significantly acts as a clearing house guiding these people in whatever direction seems appropriate.

The scheme has only been running currently for a period of 4 or 5 months so no data are available. In terms of the experience with the scheme so far, most of the people who have taken up this option come from socio-economic class E. These addicts are living under poor conditions; many of them in squats and few of them have jobs. About half of them were charged with non drug offences, so we are contacting those that we were hoping to reach and not merely those with drugs related offences. These other offences have varying degrees of relationship to their drug taking. Three quarters of them have previously been convicted so they are already involved in the criminal justice system. Commonly they are heroin addicts and many are taking the drug by 'chasing'. About half of the people so far have had no previous contact with any treatment agency. The purpose of the scheme is to act as a gateway for people who have had no previous therapeutic contact.

The major problem which we have had with the scheme so far is that despite the goodwill and enthusiasm, the numbers of people entering it have been very low. There have been only 17 referrals in a period of 4 or 5 months. It may well be that the current procedures are inappropriate. Perhaps simply handing people a card is insufficient. The police station is not perceived by drug takers as a trustworthy or sympathetic environment. Perhaps these people do not want help and are happy taking drugs. We have taken steps to make improvements; the scheme has been expanded from one police station to two. We are also undertaking a limited form of follow-up of some of those who have not taken advantage of the scheme to try and identify why they did not choose to take advantage of it.

REFERENCES

1 Brain Report.
2 Gossop M, Kristjansson I. Crime and personality. *British Journal of Criminology* 1977;**17**:264–73.
3 Gossop M, Roy A. Hostility, crime and drug dependence. *British Journal of Psychiatry* 1976;**130**:272–8.

PSYCHIATRY, NEGLIGENCE AND COMPENSATION

J J Bradley
Chairman of Council, Medical Protection Society,
Consultant Psychiatrist, Whittington Hospital

The psychiatrist may be involved in negligence claims involving compensation in three ways:

1. Negligence claims may be made against a psychiatrist alleging mismanagement or negligent treatment of a psychiatric patient.
2. Psychiatrists are often called upon by solicitors to assess the possible psychiatric ill effects of negligent treatment by surgeons or physicians.
3. The assessment of psychiatric effects of accidents, including RTAs, industrial and criminal injuries and, of course, disasters such as the Kings Cross and Bradford fires. This will include patients who have suffered psychological damage without physical injury.

The number of claims and the size of awards in negligence cases have both risen sharply in the last few years which has caused something of a crisis for the medical defence organisations and no doubt for commercial insurers in accident cases. Firms of solicitors specialising in compensation litigation advertise their expertise and organisations such as Action for the Victims of Medical Accidents (AVMA) provide advisory services for those who feel they have been negligently served by the medical profession. In the field of psychiatric negligence MIND also provides a legal advisory service.

Ever since medicine has been practiced doctors have been subject to the threat of blame whenever things go wrong. The margin between misjudgement and negligence is often very tenuous, and the public is nearly always more ready to blame the doctor whatever the circumstances. I might add that if cases come to trial courts tend to give the benefit of the doubt to the plaintiff rather than the defendant.

PSYCHIATRIC NEGLIGENCE

In my capacity as a psychiatric adviser to the Medical Protection Society (MPS) I have been able to make a study of 50 consecutive allegations of negligence in the care of psychiatric patients. Although psychiatrists are relatively low risk when compared with obstetricians and surgeons, claims and settlements can be as high as half a million pounds in cases where a patient has attempted suicide and then become paraplegic after falling from a window. While we continue without a no fault compensation system, compensation will only be payable if negligence can be proved against the doctor, or doctors, or the Health Authority. In practice very few cases ever reach trial in court on issues of liability, though some will do so on quantum. Of the 50 cases that I have studied not one has actually reached trial and a high proportion have been settled, though in some denial of liability has been accepted by the plaintiff. The categories in my series are as follows:

1. Suicide–18 cases.   ⎫   these two categories represent 50% of all
2. Attempted suicide–7 cases ⎬   cases.
3. Negligent use of lithium carbonate–7 cases. ⎫
4. Negligent use of other drugs–9 cases.   ⎬   32% of all cases
5. Failed diagnosis–3 cases.
6. Failure to control mentally handicapped patients–3 cases.
7. Negligent use of ECT–1 case.
8. Miscellaneous–3 cases, including one case of a transsexual who alleged negligence because he/she was refused operation.

Very little has been published in the British literature on the topic of psychiatric negligence. The American experience reflects to some extent the differences in the funding of medical practice and medical indemnity, but it is interesting to note that the categories of case in order of frequency are as follows:[1]

1. Suicide and attempted suicide.
2. Negligent treatment methods.
3. Negligent diagnosis.
4. Failure to warn of injury risk (e.g. ECT).
5. Unnecessary hospitalisation.
6. Sexual impropriety and improper handling of transference in psychotherapy.

Suicide

Suicide and attempted suicide are of course the most important categories. In recent years there have been three cases that have gone to court on liability.

1. *Parker v. Kent AHA*, 1978. A man who had suffered from schizophrenia for many years attempted suicide by stabbing himself in the stomach and was taken to a general hospital. He was later transferred to a psychiatric hospital where he leapt from the fire escape and thereafter he was paraplegic. He sued the hospital for negligence, firstly for not stopping him from getting up to the fire escape and secondly for not treating his back injury properly. Mr Justice Thesinger found there was no negligence in not stopping him, but £8000 was awarded for not treating his back injuries properly.
2. *Jarrett v. Yorkshire RHA*, 1980. A youth of 18 attempted suicide and was taken to a general hospital. While in hospital he jumped out of a window and consequently was paralysed from the chest down. He sued the hospital for negligence. Mr Justice Mustill found there was no negligence.

3. *Hyde v. Tameside AHA*, 1981. A plaintiff admitted to hospital with various pains thought he had cancer. He attempted suicide and was left paralysed. He brought an action against the Health Authority claiming his attempted suicide and injuries were caused by their negligence. At first instance the judge found for the plaintiff and awarded damages of £200 000. On Appeal this decision was reversed on the grounds that the plaintiff had failed to prove that the defendants were in breach of their duty to use reasonable skill and care. In the Court of Appeal Lord Denning commented on the criteria for assessing negligence in a medical case. The test for deciding whether or not it was negligent was whether it was such an error that a reasonably competent nurse acting with ordinary care might have made. He extended this test to apply to any professional person, saying that an error of judgement is not negligent where it is an error which a reasonably competent professional person acting with ordinary care might make. Lord Denning concluded that the policy of the law should be to discourage such actions whether the patient succeeds in his suicide or not.

From these cases it might appear that the defence organisations might deny liability more frequently. However, the majority of cases that I have studied have very definite weaknesses either in medical or nursing management. The common errors are:

– Failure to appreciate the seriousness of suicidal ideas and initiate appropriate observation.
– Failure of communication between senior and junior doctors, and with nursing staff.

Lithium Carbonate

A toxic substance which requires regular monitoring of blood levels, kidney and thyroid function, and which has to be taken regularly for many years might well provide potential for negligence actions. In fact there have been relatively few cases, but this may be due to the care with which patients and doctors are alerted to the dangers of this drug. Problems have arisen due to:

– Failure to appreciate the dangers of dehydration and concurrent use of diuretics.
– Failure to monitor thyroid and renal function.
– Poor communication between laboratory and doctors over serum lithium results.

A typical case history was that of a 44 year old obese woman who was admitted to hospital for weight reduction prior to hysterectomy. She had previously been stabilised on lithium carbonate for a manic depressive illness. On admission she was found to have hypertension and a diuretic was prescribed. She then developed diarrhoea and vomiting which was diagnosed as a 'bowel infection'. Lithium was continued in the same dosage in spite of dehydration. A serum lithium estimation was performed but the result which was very high at 3.1 mmol/l was not acted upon for three days. In this case the diarrhoea and vomiting was almost certainly due to lithium intoxication due to the diuretic and inadequate communication with the laboratory compounded the problem. The patient was left with permanent renal damage.

Benzodiazepines

These drugs were first introduced in 1960,[2] but it was not until 1984 that the BNF advised caution in prescribing because of the danger of dependence. Only three cases in my series have involved negligent management of benzodiazepine prescribing. In two cases the drug was stopped abruptly which precipitated a depressive reaction. Coincidentally, both these women patients strangled themselves with their tights. In a further case a young man was painstakingly weaned off diazepam over several months. He attended an out-patient clinic still complaining of anxiety and tension. He was seen for the first time by an inexperienced SHO in the out-patient department, who then prescribed lorazepam on which the patient then became dependent.

There has been a growing awareness of the large number of patients dependent upon benzodiazepines and there is now a movement resulting in application for disclosure of records to investigate possible negligent prescribing (mainly in general practice) which might result in a substantial number of claims in the future.

Negligent diagnosis

There are 3 cases in my series:

- Hodgkin's disease in a known neurotic patient under stress who suffered from lassitude, anorexia and weight loss which were not promptly investigated.
- A spinal tumour in a 23 year old unhappy youth presented as 'psychogenic backache'. There was a comment by a psychiatrist after examining the patient, 'He seemed to find it difficult to accept any psychological explanation for his symptoms—perhaps he is too naive to benefit from psychotherapy'.
- 'Psychogenic vomiting' and difficulty in swallowing for two and a half years in a 19 year old young man. He was later found to have achalasia of the cardia which was cured by operation. To be fair to the psychiatrist there were many positive psychiatric features present, but investigations were delayed.

It is perhaps heartening to note that there were only 3 cases in my series which may help put paid to the myth that psychiatrists are slow to diagnose organic disorders.

Mental Health Act

Despite the apparent potential for negligence litigation neither the 1959, nor the 1983 Mental Health Acts seems to have generated many claims. This may be accounted for by the close monitoring of the implementation of the Act by the Hospital Managers, Mental Health Review Tribunals and the Mental Health Act Commission. Additionally Section 139 of the Act allows for no civil or criminal proceedings unless a doctor has acted in bad faith or without reasonable care. No civil proceedings can be brought without leave of the High Court and no criminal proceedings without the consent of the Director of Public Prosecutions.

Incidentally, in 2 of the suicide cases that I have studied negligence was alleged because the psychiatrist *failed* to detain the patient under the Mental Health Act.

The effect of wrongful admission under the Act may well seriously affect a person's future life, quite apart from the distress of being unnecessarily detained, and claims arising from such cases could well attract substantial damages if it can be proved that doctors have acted negligently. A case of alleged unlawful detention under the 1959 Act has been reported in detail by the Medical Defence Union.[3] In this case a GP who had had previous acquaintance with a young man who had shown violent and aggressive behaviour signed a Section 26 (equivalent to the current Section 3) with a psychiatrist when the patient's behaviour had deteriorated. Their actual examination of the patient was limited because of the patient's lack of co-operation, but they felt that admission was justified because of the previous history. The patient did not show psychotic symptoms on admission, but was detained for two weeks for further observation. Unlawful detention was alleged and he was eventually allowed to bring an action, and the case came to trial in October, 1986, and the plaintiff elected for a trial by jury. After a ten day hearing the jury retired for three hours and returned their verdict that:

- The patient was not mentally ill.
- The psychiatrist was not negligent.
- The GP was not negligent.

Negligent use of ECT

Although general allegations about psychiatrists using ECT excessively are not infrequent, specific negligence claims are not common either in this country or the United States. There was only 1 case in my series in which a patient was given ECT while suffering from an upper respiratory tract infection and developed pneumonia. Strictly speaking this was a case of anaesthetic rather than psychiatric negligence.

Psychotherapy

Up to 1983 at least there were no reported damages granted for negligent psychotherapy in the USA where many more patients are prepared to invest large amounts of money in psychotherapy and psychoanalysis. However, there is a case reported in the New England Journal of Medicine in 1984[4] of a

61

patient who was also a doctor who was awarded $250 000 against a psycho-analytically orientated hospital which did not use physical methods of treatment. He alleged he was suffering from a 'biological depression' and had been denied appropriate antidepressant drugs. He then went to another hospital where these drugs were given and he then recovered.

The sole reported case in the British literature was that of a *Landau v. Werner* in 1961. A middle-aged woman discontinued treatment with a psychotherapist because she believed she had fallen in love with him. He maintained a social relationship with her as he felt that abrupt discontinuation of therapy would be harmful. The encounters upset the patient and her condition deteriorated. She claimed damages and the court ruled in her favour.

In the above case there was no suggestion of a sexual relationship which would of course attract disciplinary action from the GMC. Although there are those that have tried to advocate a physical sexual relationship between patient and therapist, it is internationally agreed that such activity is unethical and likely to be psychologically damaging rather than therapeutic. However, an anonymous national survey[5] of 1314 psychiatrists in the USA in 1986 revealed that 84 (6.4%) admitted to sexual contact with their patients, though it is not revealed whether such contact was meant to be part of the treatment.

There is a cautionary tale about social (rather than sexual) relationships with patients and prescribing. A psychiatrist was asked by his squash partner to prescribe something for his insomnia. This man was known to have had bouts of mania apparently well controlled with lithium. To oblige him the doctor gave him a week's supply of sodium amytal 400 mg, chloral 1 mg, flunitrazepam 4 mg, nitrazepam 10 mg, diazepam 10 mg, thioridazine 25 mg. After taking this cocktail one evening the patient wandered around in his garden, fell over and apparently ruptured his biceps. He then sued the doctor for negligent prescribing.

COMPENSATION

If a patient can show that he or she has suffered injury—whether physical or psychological—due to a negligent act, compensation may be payable either by the negligent individual, by some form of insurance, or by the State. There is little evidence to support the view that plaintiffs deliberately maintain or falsify symptoms to obtain higher awards, though the possibility of financial reward must inevitably act as an unconscious reinforcing factor. The robust view taken by Miller in his Milroy Lecture in 1961[6] that most minor head injury cases (and by extension most accident neuroses) claiming compensation were malingerers has not been borne out by subsequent research.[7] However, the process of litigation rather than avarice may well be an added stress and serve as an additional perpetuating factor. There may be delays of several years between the original injury and court hearing or settlement, and there is no doubt that many patients may become entrenched in a sick role reinforced by relatives, friends and even doctors. Particularly in industrial and road traffic accident cases a person may be sent to a variety of specialists instructed by the opposing sides, which only serves to force the patient into a defensive position, especially when interviewed by a doctor instructed by the defendants. Such examinations will also tend to concentrate attention on his disabilities which may become a focus for other unrelated problems. The anxiety, depression, resentment and uncertainty engendered by the long process of litigation, with or without symptoms of an underlying physical injury, will all tend to perpetuate a post traumatic neurosis. If and when compensation is finally agreed, it may come as an anti-climax and the money just allowed to remain in the bank, or very occasionally it may be treated like a football pool win and used profligately. Structured settlements instead of lump sum payment may be less traumatic psychologically.

Many cases are settled out of court, generally to the satisfaction of all parties, but a few patients feel cheated by not being allowed to express their feelings about those they feel have injured them in a public forum.

Unhappily, while we continue with an adversarial system with experts being instructed by plaintiff and defendant there may be a tendency, even among the most objective of psychiatrists, to a bias in favour of the one who pays the fees.

Solicitors acting for defendants may have somewhat unrealistic expectations of the psychiatrist they instruct by asking us to assess or even quantify exaggerations of symptoms, or to determine whether a patient is a liar or a malingerer. There is in fact a not fully validated questionnaire known as the Conscious Exaggeration Scale which is said to be helpful in differentiating the conscious from the neurotic exaggeration.[8] Some solicitors or insurance companies go to the lengths of employing private enquiry agents to monitor whether an injury causes as much disability as alleged.

PSYCHIATRIC SEQUELAE OF MEDICAL OR SURGICAL NEGLIGENCE

Assessment of the psychiatric sequelae in patients who allege negligent medical or surgical treatment will obviously cover a wide range, but as one might expect, cosmetic surgery such as face lifts, hair transplants and breast augmentations are high on the list, even though cosmetic surgeons are very well aware of the need to give pre-operative counselling and try to correct some of the extravagant expectations that patients will have for these procedures and to assess whether the patient has a body image disorder or delusion.

Necessarily, patients undergoing Caesarean section require a light anaesthetic, but there have been a number of cases in which patients allege that they have been aware during the whole operation, which must indeed be a terrifying experience, and it is often followed by phobic and depressive reactions. An organisation known as AIMS (Action for Improvement of Maternity Services) and firms of solicitors specialising in such cases are encouraging claims for awareness.

When making a psychiatric assessment a question that will need answering is whether the medical or surgical procedure, even if it has been negligently performed, is the whole cause of a patient's symptoms, or whether unrelated stress factors are operating to produce and perpetuate a neurotic reaction. In all such compensation assessments it must be remembered (particularly if one is instructed by the defendants) that vulnerability of the personality is no defence. This is known as the 'egg-shell skull principle'.[9] A patient suffering from such a syndrome with an abnormally fragile skull may be severely injured by a tap on the head. Such a plaintiff would be entitled to damages (if that tap could be shown to be negligent) commensurate with the severity of the injury that he has received. I have seen psychiatrists stand up in the witness box in a valiant attempt to reduce the amount of damages awarded and swearing on oath that the patient had an excessively vulnerable personality before the accident on the assumption that compensation would be reduced or denied, whereas the judge probably awarded even higher damages.

INJURIES AND DISASTERS

Head, back and neck injuries following industrial or traffic accidents are common and a common cause for compensation litigation. Until a few years ago surgeons and neurologists tended to assume that the problem must be psychiatric if no physical cause for persistent symptoms could be readily elicited. However, the tide of opinion seems to be changing and there is recognition that many symptoms following soft tissue injuries and minor head injuries do in fact have an organic basis.[10] Psychiatrists will still be asked to try and assess secondary neurotic symptoms, whether physical symptoms are 'exaggerated', and to give an opinion as regards prognosis of those symptoms that are considered to be 'psychiatric'. Factors indicating a poor prognosis are said to be:[11]

(a) If the patient is female.
(b) Immigrant.
(c) With over-protective relatives.
(d) Loss of libido.
(e) History of back injury.

There is immediate sympathy for those who have been caught up in major disasters that are well publicised, as evidenced by the generous response of the public to appeals, and compensation claims are generally dealt with relatively quickly, at least on an interim basis. Phobic anxiety and depressive reactions after exposure to a disaster, which may also involve bereavement and physical injury, may persist for two or three years in the most stable individuals whether claims are settled or not. Both psychosocial and neurophysiological factors are recognised as of importance in determining the symptomatology of victims exposed to acute and chronic extreme stress.[12] A study of 469 Australian fire fighters involved in a bush fire disaster in 1983[13] showed the chronicity of morbidity was related more to previous personality and past history of psychiatric illness, rather than to the severity of the exposure. However, on the egg-shell skull principle higher awards would be justified in those whose symptoms persist because of pre-existing vulnerability of the personality.

64

REFERENCES

1 Slawson P F, Guggenheim F G. Psychiatric Malpractice: A Review of the National Loss Experience. *Am J Psychiatry* 1984;**141**(8):979—81.
2 BMA General Medical Services Committee: Guidance on Benzodiazepines. September, 1988.
3 O'Donovan C. Mental Health Act—alleged unlawful detention. *Journal of MDU* 1987;17–8.
4 Stone A A. The New Paradox of Psychiatric Malpractice. *N Engl J Med* 1984; **311**(21):1384–7.
5 Gartrell N, Hernan J, Olarte S, Feldstein M, Localio R. *Am J Psychiatry* 1986;**143**: 1126–31.
6 Miller H. Accident Neurosis. *Br Med J* 1961;**1**:919–25.
7 Kelly R, Smith B N. Post Traumatic Syndrome: Another myth discredited. *J R Soc Med* 1981;**74**:275–8.
8 Clayer J R, Bookless C, Ross M W. Neurosis and Conscious Symptom Exaggeration: Its differentiation by the illness behaviour questionnaire. *J Psychosom Res* 1984;**28**: 3:237–41.
9 Dulieu v. White (1901) 2 K.B. 669, 679, per Kennedy J.
10 Porter K M. Neck Sprains After Car Accidents: A common cause of long term disability. *Br Med J* 1989;**289**:973:4.
11 Cohen R I. Post Traumatic Stress Disorder: Does it clear up when litigation is settled? *Br J of Hospital Med* 1987;485.
12 Watson I P B, Hoffman L, Wilson G V. The Neuropsychiatry of Post-Traumatic Stress Disorder. *Brit J Psychiatry* 1988;**152**:164–73.
13 McFarlane A C. The Aetiology of Post-Traumatic Morbidity: predisposing, precipitating and perpetuating factors. *Brit J Psychiatry* 1989;**154**:221–8.

GENERAL DISCUSSION

Audience   Dr Johns, your data showed that some 92% of magistrates thought that a probation order with a condition of treatment would be an effective way of helping drug offenders. You then went on to postulate that those who had a history of criminal offences prior to drug dependency would be less likely to respond well to probation. There is in fact a little evidence available to the contrary. A study I performed in the mid 1970s with a group of Charing Cross patients suggested that criminality in men was irrelevant and that they did as well as those who had not committed an offence prior to drug dependence.[1] One should not be discouraged from accepting patients for treatment as a condition of a probation order just because they have a history of criminal convictions prior to becoming dependent on drugs.

Dr Johns   I think there is a need for a properly designed research study of this important area. The magistrates may well be seeking this form of probation order, but it is clearly not going to come about without the co-operation of both the probation service and some of the treatment agencies.

Dr Eastman   I have a general question for those who spoke about drugs in prisons. I wonder whether it is the case that the objectives of the criminal justice system, including the prisons, are actually opposed to the objectives of the public health system in relation to HIV? I am particularly thinking of the inability of the Home Office to acknowledge that homosexuality occurs in prisons and therefore there should be condoms available. I wonder if it is possible to make any sort of technically based statement about the relative risk of sending a drug abuser to prison in terms of acting as a bridgehead into the community, as opposed to the risk of leaving him out in the community?

Dr Strang   I am sure you are right in drawing attention to the fact that there is considerable incompatibility in terms of the purpose behind the different approaches. There would seem to be anecdotal evidence of drug users engaging in high HIV risk activities while in the prison setting, which they would not normally engage in. There was a letter published in the BMJ by our unit about a walk-in clinic where somebody came in with advanced HIV disease whose only discernible risk behaviour was sharing needles and syringes in prison two years ago—the only occasion he had ever shared.[2] We hear reports of quite a number of people who have engaged in atypical drug and sexual behaviour in prison. I do not have any anecdotal evidence about sexual behaviour, perhaps because of the context in which I see people they are much less likely to discuss that. The extent to which the prison medical service can provide competent medical care within a system not actually geared to providing medical care is going to be an important issue over the next year or so. There would appear to be more constructive discussion going on in the prison medical service about the extent to which treatment opportunity should be considered. The real test

66

will be its actual availability and delivery and the perception of that by drug users entering the system.

Audience   This question is for Dr Bradley, it is particularly related to the question of responsibility and negligence and liability claims. In our unit there is an 18 year old lady who is moderately handicapped with an IQ of around 44 who functions socially at the age of about 6 years. Several psychiatrists have assessed her and the unanimous decision is that she is not suffering from any form of mental illness. She sporadically poses behaviour problems whilst living at home in the community. She has assaulted the neighbours, her parents and grandparents. The social services believe that she should be in a Health Authority bed, whereas the Health Authority refuse her because we do not think she is mentally ill. The questions are:

- Are we being negligent or are we liable if we do not provide a place for respite, knowing that she is not mentally ill?
- The social services and the other local authorities refuse to become involved because they feel that the person is mentally ill and the Health Authority managers refuse to provide a place, if somebody is harmed, who would be liable or negligent?

Dr Bradley   There is a possibility that she may be, within the meaning of the Act, mentally impaired. That is a clinical decision and it is not just based on IQ alone. If she is mentally impaired and ought to be detained, then that is for two doctors and a social worker or nearest relative to make the application under Section 3. If you believe that she ought to be in hospital and the Health Authority will not have her, then the Health Authority would have to take that responsibility. If none of you believe that she ought to be in hospital and she is behaving in a manner that is irresponsible or dangerous to other people, then the law would apply to her like anybody else, and if she assaults somebody, then she could be taken to court.

REFERENCES

1 d'Orban P T. Criminality as a prognostic factor in opiate dependence. *Br J Psychiat* 1975;**127**:86–9.
2 Strang J, Orgel M, Farrell M. Well users clinic for drug users. *Br Med J* 1989;**298**: 1310.

LIST OF DELEGATES
PSYCHIATRY AND THE LAW
26th May 1989

Dr G P Adams London	Mr G Boyle Goodmayes	Dr C C Cordess London
Dr R C Adams Isle of Wight	Dr N D Brener London	Dr D P Cronin Brentwood
Dr M J Akhtar South Shields	Dr G W K Bridge York	Dr S Crown London
Dr D Allen Reading	Dr H Bullard Wallingford	Dr J M R Damas-Mora Sunderland
Dr R P Arya Southport	Dr L S Cantlay Cleveland	Dr P Danuta Peterborough
Dr J R Attah Derby	Dr R Caplan Lincoln	Dr N Datt London
Dr A Balasubramaniam Gloucester	Mr K Caraballo London	Dr C Davies Bath
Dr V T Baraniecka Middlesex	Dr S K Chakravarti Huddersfield	Dr K W de Pauw Leicester
Dr P Barczak Lincoln	Dr T G Chand Chorley	Dr N M Desai Nuneaton
Dr A Bartlett London	Dr J C C Chase Hertfordshire	Dr V C Devakumar Rossendale
Dr D A Bennett Basingstoke	Dr S Chattree Blackburn	Ms L Dillistone London
Mr W Bingley London	Dr A Cheyne Northumberland	Mr P J Donkin Newcastle-upon-Tyne
Dr J M Bishop Kent	Dr S Chhabra Jarrow	Dr P T D'Orban London
Dr A A Black London	Dr J I Coleman Worcester	Dr R Driscoll London
Dr M Blackburn Horsham	Dr C G Conway Yealmpton	Dr J Dunn London
Dr N Bouras London	Dr A Copello London	Dr V Edward Aberdeen

Dr H G Egdell
North Yorkshire

Dr A A El Komy
Chichester

Dr H Etkin
West Sussex

Dr M S Evans
South Glamorgan

Dr M Farrell
London

Dr E Fernando
Kent

Dr J D W Fisher
Sevenoaks

Dr M W Fowles
Norwich

Mr R Fream
Surrey

Dr K W M Fulford
Oxford

Dr J Gavilan
London

Dr M George
Birmingham

Dr C Ghosh
Crowthorne

Dr S K Ghosh
Hereford

Dr J O Gonzalez
Sleaford

Dr R Goodwin
Brentwood

Dr B Green
Prescot

Dr N Gunther
Middlesex

Dr K M Hadi
Stevenage

Dr J Hajioff
St Albans

Dr A Hall
Warlingham

Dr M Hammond
Caterham

Dr S Haque
Essex

Dr I Harvey
London

Dr J L Hertzog
Portsmouth

Ms A Hill
Ascot

Dr Hindson
London

Dr S C Hollins
London

Dr A H I Hourani
Birmingham

Dr S E Hoyes
Rotherham

Dr K Hussain
Newcastle

Dr M F Hussain
Canterbury

Mr S Hutchison
London

Dr R W Huws
Sheffield

Dr G S Ibrahimi
London

Dr S A Iles
Wallingford

Dr V Iyer
Hull

Dr M G A Izmeth
Southport

Dr A K Jain
Stockport

Dr D James
London

Dr C Jarman
London

Mrs H Johnson
Dagenham

Dr R Judge
Worcester

Dr S R Kadambari
London

Dr G Kanagaratnam
Chichester

Dr S E Kanagaratnam
Chichester

Dr S A Karim
Chester

Dr A Katz
Barnet

Dr W E S Kiernan
London

Mrs J Korgaontar
Hatfield

Dr H A W Krekorian
Buckingham

69

Dr K I Kumar Bedford	Dr B M Male Chichester	Dr N Murando Cwmbran
Dr H Kurmoo Coventry	Mr B Malin Croydon	Mrs J Neal Luton
Dr M Lakatos Slough	Dr J Marks Cheltenham	Dr M J Nettleship Derby
Dr E P Larkin Notts	Dr H Masih York	Mr S Obcarskas London
Ms K Law Epsom	Dr D R Master London	Mr F O'Connor Surrey
Dr H M J Leegood London	Dr G Mathew St Albans	Mrs J O'Connor Surrey
Dr A G Lewis London	Dr J Mathews Blackburn	Dr T J O'Grady Lincoln
Dr J M Lomax-Simpson London	Dr S C Mathews Cwmbran	Dr M O'Rourke Bedfordshire
Dr K Loucas Crowthorne	Dr D C Mawson Maghull	Dr M O'Rourke Chichester
Dr D I Lowe Sevenoaks	Dr C T Methven Gloucester	Dr A Orwin Edgbaston
Dr M Lowe Essex	Dr I H Mian Bristol	Dr P Page Cheltenham
Dr J M McCarthy Ilford	Mr T Middleton Harlow	Dr M A Palejwala Walsall
Dr H J McKee London	Dr H Mogallupu Maghull	Dr S Parameshwaran London
Dr A A McKirdy West Sussex	Dr D H Montgomery Epsom	Dr A L Parker Crawley
Dr I McLoughlin Newcastle	Mr A Mooniaruck Harlow	Dr D Parker Oxford
Dr I Macquire-Samson Bristol	Dr R K Mudaliar Northampton	Dr J M Parrott Kent
Dr S K Majumdar Kent	Dr M Munir Gloucester	Dr C Parry London

70

Mr R Pathmanathan
Harlow

Mr D Pearson
Leek

Dr N Pearson
Fareham

Dr A Perez
Northampton

Dr M M Perez
Camberley

Dr A J Peters
London

Dr R J Pether
London

Dr R C Peveler
Oxford

Dr C J Porter
Manchester

Dr E F Prah
Haywards Heath

Dr M S R Prasad
Hull

Dr R Preston
Milton Keynes

Dr M Quasim
Nuneaton

Dr M J H Qureshi
Wolverhampton

Dr E A Ragheb
Birmingham

Dr M Z Rahman
Glasgow

Dr T Rajamanickam
Burnley

Dr D Rajapakse
Colchester

Dr H A N Ranasinghe
Cheshire

Dr T Rasamuthiah
Luton

Dr P M Raucheubey
Birmingham

Dr S Reddy
Essex

Dr A Regan
Bucks

Mr H Richards
Edinburgh

Dr C E Riley
London

Dr D A Robertson
Fairlie

Dr J R Robertson
Epsom

Dr A A Robin
Surrey

Dr P Rohde
London

Dr J W Rollins
Gosport

Dr R J R Ropner
Cheltenham

Dr H K Rose
Purley

Dr P K Roy
Suffolk

Dr M Sabaratnam
Colchester

Dr B N Saha
Chertsey

Dr Salem
Lincoln

Dr W Samarasinghe
Herts

Dr G S Sarna
Notts

Dr Sathy
Surrey

Dr S Sellaturay
Herts

Dr S M T Serafi
Cheshire

Dr S H Shariff
Doncaster

Dr G C Shetty
Maghull

Dr S Shivanathan
Kent

Dr A K Sinha
Sheffield

Dr T Sriranganathan
Taunton

Mr I Stanier
London

Dr N J Suffling
Poole

Dr R Summers
Caterham

Dr S Swierczynski
Chertsey

Dr T K Szulecka
Worksop

Dr R Tamby
Bedford

Dr M J Tarsh
Harrow

Dr R Theva
Caterham

Dr R M Toms
Colchester

Dr K L K Trick
Northampton

Mrs D Trike

Dr M Twomey
Carlisle

Dr B Upadhyay
Leek

Dr J Van der Knapp
London

Dr A N Varma
Sleaford

Miss F Vernon
Warlingham

Dr D Waniga-Ratner
London

Mr A R Welch
Harrow

Mr B Wickett
Harlow

Dr G C Wijesiri
Crumpsall

Mrs S Wiltshire
Epsom

Dr I R Wood
Aylesbury

Dr S M Wood
Retford

Dr M E F Woollaston
Marlborough

Dr S Wright
Sheffield

Dr A Wylie
Caterham

Dr N M Yousufzai
Walsall

Dr M A Zaman
Derby

MEDICAL RELATIONS PUBLICATIONS

CURRENT APPROACHES SERIES

Vertigo   (reprinted October 1985)

Small Bowel Disease

Endometrial Carcinoma

Risk/Benefits of Antidepressants

Obesity

Affective Disorders in the Elderly

Childbirth as a Life Event

Sleep Disorders

Advances in Pancreatitis

Sudden Cardiac Death

Neuropsychiatric Aspects of AIDS

Stress, Immunity and Disease

The Problem of Recurrent Abdominal Pain

Breaking Bad News

Mental Retardation

The above publications can be obtained by writing to:
DUPHAR MEDICAL RELATIONS
Duphar Laboratories Limited
West End
Southampton
SO3 3JD